North C

OFF THE B

"Includes tips on best places to eat and sleep, little known gems, and how to bypass the tourist traps."

—*The Salisbury Post* (N.C.)

"Fascinating reading . . . . a melange of sites, restaurants, lodgings, and directions leading to the author['s] personal choices. Lovingly written . . . enthusiastically testif[ies] to the old notion about seeing America first."

—*Booklist,* American Library Association

"Reveals features [that] will attract even those who had not planned on ever visiting the state. When they do, this will be the handbook to choose."

—Midwest Book Review

"The off-the-beaten-path traveler is assured of enjoying these discoveries as much as the author did."

—*Bookpage*

"Ms. Pitzer writes with enthusiasm and knowledge. When she says someplace is worth visiting, you can count on it."

—*The State,* (Columbia, S.C.)

"When you're accompanied by *North Carolina: Off the Beaten Path,* it's like having your own personal tour guide."

—*Southern Living*

North Carolina

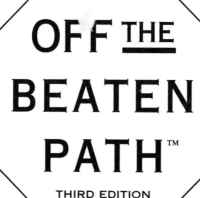

OFF THE
BEATEN
PATH™

THIRD EDITION

SARA PITZER

A Voyager Book

The
Globe
Pequot
Press

Old Saybrook, Connecticut

Cover map copyright © DeLorme Mapping
Illustrations by Carole Drong

Library of Congress Cataloging-in-Publication Data
Pitzer, Sara.
  North Carolina : off the beaten path / Sara Pitzer. — 3rd ed.
    p. cm. — (Off the beaten path series)
  "A voyager book."
  Includes index.
  ISBN 1-56440-746-2
  1. North Carolina—Guidebooks. I. Title. II. Series.
F252.3.P58   1996
917.5604'43—dc20   96-2474
                                                            CIP

Manufactured in the United States of America
Third Edition/First Printing

This is for Judy.
She gave me a house so I'm giving her a book.
I really needed a house.
I don't think Judy needs a book ,
but it's the best I can do.

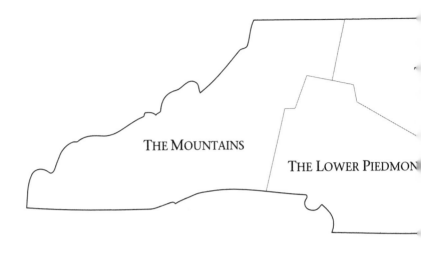

THE MOUNTAINS

THE LOWER PIEDMON

NORTH CAROLINA

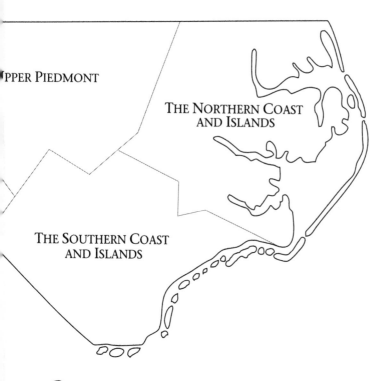

PPER PIEDMONT

THE NORTHERN COAST
AND ISLANDS

THE SOUTHERN COAST
AND ISLANDS

CONTENTS

ACKNOWLEDGMENTS

Many of the photographs from which the drawings in this book were made were provided by the North Carolina Division of Travel and Tourism.

Thanks to Mickey Smith and Terry Almond at the Richfield Post Office for providing information about Portsmouth Island. Thanks to John and Elizabeth Sturgeon for telling me about Casar, a town no tourist is likely to find normally. Thanks to the Williamsons at Ocean Isle for arranging a place off the beaten path for me to stay year after year. Thanks to the people at Jay Howard's studio in Charlotte for keeping me abreast of changes in that city. And, most of all, thanks to the scores of kind North Carolinians who gave me directions, marked my maps, and on occasion actually led me to the proper road all the considerable number of times I got lost.

INTRODUCTION

I was lost—again—somewhere around Raleigh, but nowhere near the place I wanted to be. I'd already pulled into the entrance of a large industrial park, where an executive stopped on his way out to ask if he could help me. I'd already walked along the sidewalk in front of North Carolina State University, where a professor leaving campus gave me detailed instructions on getting out of the city in the direction I wanted to go. And I was pretty sure I was going to get it right, if I could just find the beltway. Seeing that the car in the next lane had both windows down as we waited for a light to turn, I called across to the driver, "Is this road going to take me to the beltway?"

"Where do you want to go?" he yelled back. I told him. "Follow me," he shouted, and when the light changed, took off in a cloud of exhaust. I followed him nearly 10 miles. At the proper entrance onto the beltway, he blinked his turn signal and also pointed emphatically with his left hand, just in case I missed the signal. I turned. He was already gone, leaving me with a grin and a wave.

And that's how people in North Carolina are.

For me, living in North Carolina is no accident of birth or whim of corporate transfer; it's a studied choice. When my husband and I decided that we should both work freelance, it meant that we could live pretty much wherever we wanted to. We spent the better part of a year looking for a place where the topography was appealing, the climate was sunny and temperate, the economy was thriving, and the people were nice. We found North Carolina.

In the years since we moved here in 1983, life has been one joyful discovery about the state after another. Indeed, sometimes it seems too good to believe. Many mornings I wake up thinking: Today's the day I'm going to be disappointed. But I never am.

In 1993 my husband Croy died with ALS (Lou Gherig's Disease). In a way it was the happiest year of his life. Although his body deteriorated, his mind did not, so he knew and understood every day the remarkable friendship and love that our North Carolina friends, neighbors, and business associates showered upon him without restraint. The last photograph ever taken of him, a week before he died, shows Croy sitting by our pool in the sun at the edge of the woods, surrounded by his friends. The sky was Carolina blue, the people were joking, and everybody, including

Croy, was laughing. He often said, "This is the most wonderful place on earth." And that day, after sharing a decade of discoveries in North Carolina, we knew it was more true than ever.

I'm making the discoveries on my own now. It tells you a lot about North Carolina that there are still lots of laughing friends around, and that the experience continues to delight me. I know you'll enjoy my discoveries, too.

Take the barbecue, for instance. Two authors writing an article on southern barbecue for *Cook's* magazine traveled through several states looking for the best barbecue restaurants, but they were not able to get to North Carolina. They apologized in their article, because, they said, in comparison, nothing else is barbecue at all. (North Carolina barbecue is always pork cooked over a wood fire, never prepared in a sauce, and usually served with slaw and hush puppies.)

Then there's the pottery. This state has scores and scores of potters, working in the historic old production styles and in contemporary studio modes, producing such a variety of work that a collection could easily crowd everything else from a room.

As for topography, North Carolina has some of the oldest mountains in the world, the largest natural sand dune on the East Coast, and some of the most unspoiled beaches and islands in the country. The rich soil of the Piedmont and foothills grows apples, vegetables, Christmas trees, cotton, and tobacco, a problematic crop with much historic significance.

Also historically important, North Carolina, one of the thirteen original colonies, played important roles in the Revolutionary War, the Civil War, and World Wars I and II. The area is rich in Indian history; blacks made many early significant advances here; and the Moravians created a historic settlement at Old Salem. The Wright brothers first accomplished powered flight in North Carolina, on a site that is popular today with hang gliders more interested in playing than in setting records.

Each of the three major geographic areas of the state—the coastal plain, the Piedmont, and the mountains—differs radically from the others. It's almost like traveling through three smaller states. The nature of each region influenced the kinds of commerce that flourished historically and continue to flourish, and also left a mark on the people. As you travel, you'll hear fascinating changes in the music of the accents of people native to each region.

The coastal plain accounts for almost two-fifths of the state's area. The North Carolina coast has been considered dangerous since the first settlers tried to cope with its ever-changing beaches, currents, and waterways. There was no guarantee that just because you had safely sailed into a particular port once, you would find it safe, or even open, the next time you tried. That's at least one reason why English colonization shifted up toward the Chesapeake and why North Carolina was settled more sparsely and slowly than some other colonies were. Even today you find areas that are remarkably sparsely settled compared to most states' coastal regions. For vacationers, the main activities and sightseeing are related to the same activities that have supported the area economically—fishing, boating, and beachgoing.

In the Piedmont, which makes up about another two-fifths of the state, you find mostly rolling hills and red clay. Although the clay is harder to work than the sandy soil of the coast, it seems to have held better its fertility against some pretty bad early farming habits. (Wherever they are grown, cotton and tobacco are notorious for wearing out the soil.) Since the Piedmont doesn't have many large stretches of flat land, it didn't invite the huge plantations that had to be worked with many slaves. Smaller family farms were often worked by the people who owned them, perhaps with some hired help. The historians Hugh Talmage Lefler and Albert Ray Newsome point out in their classic *The History of a State: North Carolina* that the narrow, swift streams of the Piedmont, which weren't worth much for transportation, were great for generating power. And that, along with the presence of hardwoods and other resources, accounts for the great number of manufacturing activities that flourish in the Piedmont. Here you find lots of attractions related to manufacturing—tobacco museums, furniture showrooms, and more outlet stores than you can count. Probably because of the past concentration of moneyed manufacturers and merchants, you'll also find rich lodes of cultural attractions and arts here.

The mountains make up the smallest part of the state, but they compensate in interest and beauty for what they lack in area. Some of the highest mountains in the Appalachians are here. As anyone who drives in the mountains knows, transportation is difficult. In earlier times it was nearly impossible, hence the development of small pockets of civilization separated by stretches of wilderness, creating those tough, independent, resourceful, self-sufficient folks—mountain people. This kind of early self-sufficiency and distance from major metropolitan areas made the growth of all kinds of crafts almost inevitable. The mountains are still the richest source of handcrafts in the state.

Although tourism and technology have homogenized somewhat the state's regional populations, you can still find lots of those tall, thin, rangy people. It remains a pretty good joke in the Piedmont for a young woman marrying outside the area to claim she's found herself a mountain man.

Of course, today the immigration of Yankees from "up north" and considerable growth mean that every region has its share of developers, builders, and real estate people. These activities, however, tend to be clustered mostly around the major cities and a few popular mountain and beach resort areas. There are still lots of places off the beaten path to go for fun.

As a place to play, the state offers hiking and white-water rafting, waterskiing and snow skiing, freshwater and saltwater fishing and boating, athletics, auto racing, horseback riding, and golf on some of the most famous courses in the country.

Face it, you're not going to be able to do it all or see it all in one trip, or even in ten trips. Don't try to squeeze too much into a single trip, or you'll end up driving a lot and not doing much else. But the driving you do shouldn't be unpleasant if you avoid the interstates around major cities at rush hour and accept the fact that the two-lane roads tend to be well maintained but slow, since there are few good places for passing slow drivers and tractors. To understand the roads and decide when to travel on a major highway and when to get onto secondary roads, you'll definitely need a state map. The best one is the North Carolina transportation map, issued by the North Carolina Department of Transportation and the Division of Travel and Tourism (800–847–4862). You may pick one up free at a welcome center or receive it by writing North Carolina Division of Travel and Tourism, 430 North Salisbury Street, Raleigh 27611.

If you or those traveling with you are in any way physically challenged, you should also request a copy of the book *Access, North Carolina*. This is a remarkably good book published by the North Carolina Department of Human Resources, the Division of Vocational Rehabilitation Services, and the Division of Travel and Tourism. It briefly describes historic sites, state and national parks and forests, and general-interest attractions, focusing on their accessibility of parking, entrance, interior rooms, exterior areas, and rest rooms. The book is free.

A state with so many resources inevitably becomes the subject of many books. Depending on your interests, you may find several of them interesting to use along with this guide. The University of North Carolina Press publishes *Turners and Burners: The Folk Potters of North Carolina,* by Charles G. Zug III, the most complete explication of the subject available. The press also publishes many books about North Carolina history. For further information, write University of North Carolina Press, P.O. Box 2288, Chapel Hill 27514.

If you are a devotee of back roads, you may enjoy Earl Thollander's *Back Roads of the Carolinas,* devoted entirely to "nonhighway" drives along roads that often aren't on regular maps. Thollander designed the book, lettered the text in calligraphy, and drew the maps and wash illustrations himself. Often Thollander suggests a dirt road or other obscure route from one historic point to another, which you could use as a much, much slower alternative to the routes I suggest. It is published by Clarkson N. Potter, Inc., One Park Avenue, New York, NY 10016. Finally, the North Carolina publisher John F. Blair (1406 Plaza Drive, Winston-Salem, 27103-1485) offers several books about the history and ecology of the North Carolina coast, plus an appealing book of photographs and native comment, *Ocracoke Portrait,* by Ann Ehringhaus, whose bed-and-breakfast inn on Ocracoke appears in this guidebook. It's especially fun to read such books ahead of time and then carry them with you to consult, because the material comes alive as you see the subject matter firsthand.

With or without the books, though, North Carolina comes alive when you travel here because of its people. Significant history, appealing countryside, even good food can be part of any well-planned trip. Adding helpful, friendly, almost uniformly cheerful people changes the mix from plain cake to an angel food celebration. In the years I've been traveling almost continuously about the state, I've not had a single unpleasant experience with a North Carolinian. Unless you carry a chip the size of one of Mount Mitchell's ancient trees on your shoulder, you won't either. And if you're in that bad a mood, don't come. If you can't have fun in North Carolina, you can't enjoy yourself anywhere. Might as well stay home.

The prices and rates listed in this guidebook were confirmed at press time. We recommend, however, that you call establishments before traveling to obtain current information.

THE SOUTHERN COAST AND ISLANDS

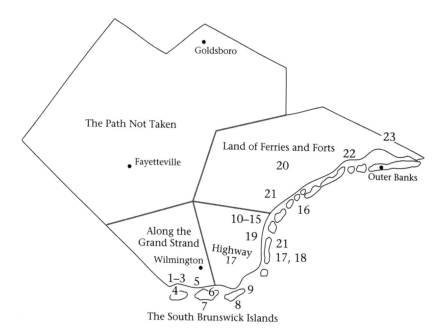

Goldsboro

The Path Not Taken

Fayetteville

Land of Ferries and Forts

23

22

20

Outer Banks

21

16

10–15

19

21

Along the Grand Strand

Highway 17

17, 18

Wilmington

1–3 5

4

6

9

7

8

The South Brunswick Islands

1. Calabash
2. Captain Jim's Marina
3. Ella's Restaurant
4. Sunset Beach
5. Italian Fisherman
6. Ocean Isle
7. Scheffield's
8. Holden Beach
9. Southport
10. Historic Wilmington District
11. St. John's Museum of Art
12. Chandler's Wharf
13. Cotton Exchange

14. USS *North Carolina* Battleship Memorial
15. *Henrietta II*
16. Wrightsville Beach
17. Fort Fisher National Historic Site
18. North Carolina Aquarium
19. Tote-em-in Zoo
20. Duplin Wine Cellars
21. Poplar Grove Plantation
22. Camp Lejeune Marine Base
23. Cedar Point

THE SOUTHERN COAST AND ISLANDS

ALONG THE GRAND STRAND

Like most of this country's coastal areas, the beaches of North Carolina attract plenty of tourists, but some have so far managed to avoid the near honky-tonk atmosphere of the better known places such as Myrtle Beach, just below the North Carolina–South Carolina border.

Close enough to that border to confuse anyone who misses the North Carolina welcome center on Highway 17, the little community of ◆ **Calabash** comes as a surprise to all but the people who visit beaches in the area regularly. The sign proclaiming Calabash the seafood capital of the world seems bigger than the town, which covers only a couple of miles and has only a couple hundred permanent residents. But you'll find more than thirty restaurants, all specializing in seafood. Mostly they're owned and run by local fishing families, are invariably casual, and feature fresh "Calabash-style" deep-fried seafood.

Calabash-style means the seafood has a light, almost tempura, batter coating. Of course it's served with hush puppies; it's easier to separate income and tax than it is to get seafood in Calabash without hush puppies. Oyster roasts are as popular as the fried seafood. When you order an oyster roast, you're presented with a huge kettle full of oysters steamed just until they open, a shucking knife to prod the oysters out of their shells, a dish of melted butter, a roll of paper towels, and a wastebasket to catch the oyster shells as you empty them.

Any number of restaurants claim to be the original Calabash restaurant and to have the authentic recipe for Calabash-style seafood. One of the most established and best is **Captain Nance's Seafood Restaurant,** on the Calabash River (which is full of shrimp, crabs, and flounder). The restaurant is open from 11:00 A.M. to 9:00 P.M. seven days a week, year-round (910–579–2574).

Nearby, also on the Calabash River, ◆ **Captain Jim's Marina** charters boats at reasonable rates for full- and half-day fishing. If you enjoy the sport but hate the mess that follows, you'll appreciate the free fish-cleaning service. And if you find the whole fishing thing just too gory for words, you're a likely customer for an evening riding cruise. Charters leave from the marina every day. If you're seriously interested in boating, you should call ahead (910–579–3660), as weather, special charters, and slow seasons can affect the regular schedule.

A smaller restaurant with a strong family feel that you might miss just driving through the area is ❖**Ella's Restaurant,** a pleasant place for seafood and a beer or soft drink. Ella's presumably has fed a full share of rainy-day customers, because the following legend is displayed near the front: COIL UP YOUR ROPES AND ANCHOR HERE / TILL BETTER WEATHER DOTH APPEAR. To get to Ella's, turn onto Highway 179, at the only red light in Calabash, heading toward the water. You can seek food or shelter from 11:00 A.M. to 10:00 P.M., seven days a week, year-round.

In the summer Calabash is very busy, attracting tourists from Myrtle Beach as well as from the beaches to the north. The marina and the better restaurants, however, operate year-round, and in slower seasons a stop in Calabash is low-key and can be fun.

THE SOUTH BRUNSWICK ISLANDS

Driving north on Highway 17 just over 10 miles takes you to the beginning of the South Brunswick Islands. Sunset Beach, Ocean Isle, and Holden Beach differ from one another as much as the siblings in most families. Part of the chain of barrier islands off the coast that stretches both north and south, the South Brunswick Islands have no boardwalks and relatively little commercial development except for beach houses and a few small grocery stores.

In the fall of 1989, Hurricane Hugo accentuated an interesting phenomenon along Holden Beach, Ocean Isle, and Sunset Beach. The hurricane didn't do any more damage than any good storm does, breaking up some docks, flooding some first-floor rooms in cabins, and lifting off a piece of roof here and there. But it moved the beaches, literally, hastening an erosion process that was already obvious, moving sand and dunes from the east and depositing them farther west. This means that beachfront at Holden Beach grows noticeably more narrow with each storm, as does the east end of Ocean Isle's beachfront, leading to black-humor jokes suggesting that the way to get an oceanfront property here is to buy third row and wait. Meanwhile the beaches on the west end of Ocean Isle and those on Sunset Beach are visibly growing more and more broad. It takes regular dredging to keep the waterway between Ocean Isle and Sunset Beach open because the currents continue to dump sand there. Beaches have broadened so much at Sunset Beach that when you stand at water's edge, you can't see the first-row cottages behind the dunes. It sounds like good, forward-thinking planning; actually, it's nature.

This shifting creates some problems for developers and homeowners but does not in any way spoil the pleasure of visiting any of the islands. Indeed, if you're interested in the ecology of coastlines, try to find a copy of *The Beaches are Moving*, by Wallace Kaufman and Orrin H. Pilkey, Jr., published by Duke University Press in 1979. The book describes, explains, and predicts such activity, though it focuses on beaches along both the east and west coasts and doesn't talk specifically about the South Brunswick Islands. Browsing through the book, which is rich in historical data and information about how tides, storms, and so on work, while you stay in the South Brunswick Islands is like having your very own little nature model to study as you read. It's great fun and genuinely instructive.

Access to ❖**Sunset Beach** still depends on a one-lane swing bridge across the Intracoastal Waterway. A swing bridge differs from a drawbridge in that the movable part of the bridge swings to the side rather than lifting up to allow tall ships to pass under. It's unique in these times. It's also threatened. Developers have plans to replace it with a higher, modern bridge that would accommodate more traffic faster. At the moment, people who like the sleepy, undeveloped atmosphere of Sunset Beach are fighting to stop the new bridge. They'll probably lose. But, at least for the immediate future, this is a place with only a few paved roads and sidewalks, no high-rise condos, and no pink giraffes or water slides or beachfront grills. What the island does have is glorious, wide, flat beaches and clean white sand. From most of the beach area, you can't see any buildings at all. The beach homes, most of which are available for rent, sit hidden behind the dunes. The best way to enjoy Sunset Beach is to rent one of these houses. They are handled by three rental agents. The newest of these, which may therefore be trying harder, is the Odom Company, which does everything from letting you go directly to your rental home instead of stopping to check in at the office to lending you crab traps and charcoal grills. The office (910–579–3515 or 910–579–6201) is open seven days a week, year-round, from 9:00 A.M. to 5:00 P.M. During the summer season cottage rentals are usually by the week, Saturday to Saturday. At other times terms are more flexible.

Also, near where the bridge comes onto the island, you can rent rooms at Continental Motel (910–579–6772).

Whether you stay awhile or just pass through, a nice place to stop for dinner is the ◆**Italian Fisherman,** on the mainland right next to the bridge that crosses the waterway to the island. The restaurant is one of the thoroughly established operations in the area that attracts customers year-round. In addition to seafood prepared with Italian seasonings, you can order several fine veal dishes, a variety of pasta dishes, and wonderful fried calamari. This is the kind of place where the same people work year after year and remember those visitors who return. Although there is a complete bar, and drinks are served in the dining rooms as well, the atmosphere is holiday casual, and entire families, including babies in high chairs, can eat comfortably here. The guests tend to be as friendly as the staff, often striking up conversations from one table to another. One summer evening an eighteen-month-old in a high chair was doing a standard smear job on her face, head, and hair with spaghetti. A diner at the next table snapped a picture of the scene and later sent it to the child's parents. The Italian Fisherman (910–579–2929) is open seven days a week during the summer season, from 5:00 to 9:00 P.M. In the off-season the restaurant is open only Wednesday through Sunday. In November the days are Thursday through Sunday. They are usually busy, so reservations are a very good idea.

The next island north is ◆**Ocean Isle.** To get there, drive north on Highway 17 about 5 miles and turn right onto Route 179 South, which takes you directly to the Odell Williamson Bridge, across the Intracoastal Waterway. The fact that the island was originally settled in 1954 by Odell and his family, who rowed across the waterway after Hurricane Hazel to get to the island, tells you something about the island. The Williamson family still runs a lively rental, sales, and building business on the island. Although there is a water slide, you'll find little other commercial development here. A few convenience shops and gift shops sell beachwear, suntan lotion, and other items tourists buy. This island is more settled, with sidewalks, all-paved roads, some cluster homes and condos on the west end, and more traditional beach homes on the east end. Also on the east end, a series of paved and natural canals, where the homes have docks, can accommodate boats or just provide pleasant off-ocean outdoor lounging space. A few hundred permanent residents live on the island. Their homes are mingled among those used strictly for vacation and rental. It's a nice mix, and especially if you do not stay in beachfront properties, you can learn a lot about the island from these people and form friendships that continue past your visit. **Williamson Realty,** one of several realtors that handle island homes, is pleasant to deal with if you want to rent a cottage or condo. Their Saturday-to-Saturday rental schedule during the season, with more flexibility at other times, operates much the same as on Sunset Beach. The office (910–579–2373 or 579–2858) is open from 9:00 A.M. to 5:00 P.M., Monday through Saturday, and Sunday from noon to 4:00 P.M. (closed on Sundays during December, January, and February). **Sloan Realty** (800–843–6044) is another well-established, friendly rental agency. Their offices are open six days a week from 9:00 A.M. to 5:00 P.M., Sundays from 10:00 to 4:00 P.M., except June 2 to September 1, when hours are 12:30 to 5:00 P.M.

Ocean Isle Inn (800–352–5988) rents nice waterfront motel rooms by the night.

Whatever you do while you're at Ocean Isle, spend some time at ◆**Scheffield's.** It has a boat dock in back, automobile gas pumps in front, groceries, fishing supplies, and beer inside, and the nicest people imaginable everywhere. You can buy just-caught shrimp and fish, newly dug clams, all the fixin's to go with them, and in the process, trade recipes with the proprietors for preparing whatever you bought. Scheffield's (910–579–2574) is open from 7:30 A.M. to 9:00 P.M. (10:00 P.M. on weekends) seven days a week, year-round.

Standing on the west end of Ocean Isle, you can see Sunset Beach. It looks close enough to wade over, which old-timers remember doing before erosion and currents changed the shape of the islands. Standing on the east end of Ocean Isle, you see ◆**Holden Beach,** also seeming almost close enough to wade across. Without a boat, though, getting to Holden Beach takes a drive of about fifteen minutes. Richard Mubel, the news editor for the *State Port Pilot,* once wrote for the *Brunswick Magazine* that Holden is a place where "old meets new, where tradition bisects progress and where history intersects the path of the future." He's talking about the contrasts between the back side of the island, along the Atlantic Intracoastal Waterway and the Lockwood Folly River Inlet, and the oceanfront. Shrimpers and anglers descended from families who settled the area still work along the waterway and inlet, as well as in the open sea, but the oceanfront is strictly a vacationland of white beaches and summer cottages. You'll find more shopping in this area, but compared to major coastal resort areas, it's still quiet and appeals to people who like a little more activity than can be found at Sunset or Ocean Isle without getting into plastic, chrome, and glass. Half a dozen rental agents renting cottages and condos, a campground, and a motel serve the area. **Alan Holden Realty** (800–720–2200) has the most properties and friendly people to answer the phone. They're open from 9:00 A.M. to 5:00 P.M., seven days a week, year-round. The **Gray Gull Motel** (910–842–6775), an older but clean establishment, rents individual rooms. They, too, operate year-round. This small motel is located between the light and the bridge where you first drive onto the island.

If you enjoy local festivals and if you lo-o-o-o-ve seafood, try to schedule your Brunswick Island trip for the third weekend in October, for the annual **North Carolina Oyster Festival.** This festival began as a small oyster roast in the late 1970s. Every year the party got a little better and in three years got itself proclaimed the official oyster festival of North Carolina. It takes a couple hundred community volunteers to run the event, which now includes a beach run, a bullshooting (tall-tale–telling) contest, and the North Carolina Oyster Shucking Championship. This contest is no small potatoes. It has produced not only a national oyster shucking champion, but also the top female oyster shucker in the world. With all that shucking going on, it stands to figure somebody's got to be doing some eating. That's where you come in. Steamed oysters, fried oysters, oysters on the half shell, boiled shrimp, fried flounder, and of course the ubiquitous hush puppies are available in abundance. Food is served from noon to 7:00 P.M. on Saturday and, on a more limited scale, from 1:00 to 5:00 P.M. on Sunday. In addition to the food and contests, the festival features two days of live music that include beach music (shag), top forty, country and western, and gospel. Also artists and craftspeople display their wares for sale. For fuller details and firm dates in any year, call the South Brunswick Islands Chamber of Commerce (910–754–6644).

HIGHWAY 17

The Brunswick Isles are served by businesses in the town of **Shalotte,** a few miles inland on Highway 17. This is the place to stop when you need to do laundry or pick up a bicycle pump from the hardware store or get a prescription filled in a good-sized pharmacy. From Shalotte, driving north on Highway 17 for a little less than an hour brings you to Wilmington. On the way you should take a little side trip to ◆**Southport,** on the western bank of the Cape Fear River where the river joins the Atlantic Ocean. The town, rich in military and maritime history, was first called Smithville after Benjamin Smith, who became governor of North Carolina, but in 1887 the name was changed to Southport. To get into town from Highway 17, turn right onto State Highway 211. Shortly you'll be driving into what is obviously still a real fishing village with stores and gas stations and marinas that look functional rather than prettily gentrified. Many of the homes in Southport are listed on the National Register of Historic Places. Although the word "quaint" is overused, it pertains here. For instance the old twelve-bed **Fort Johnston Hospital,** dating back to about 1852, has been moved and turned into a private residence; the **Old Brunswick Jail,** dating back to the early 1900s, now houses the Southport Historical Society. In the **Keziah Memorial Park** you find a tree that the Cape Fear Indians bent over as a marker when it was just a sapling. It may be more than 800 years old. Half a century ago children could crawl under its arch. And the **A. E. Stevens House,** circa 1894, is noted as the home built for Mr. Stevens and his betrothed. She changed her mind and married his best friend. They built a house across from Mr. Stevens, who remained a bachelor the rest of his life. There's lots more, equally human and interesting, all mapped out on a one-mile, self-guided walking tour called **Southport Trail.** You'll find a nice assortment of restaurants, antiques shops, and specialty stores in the area, too. Their names and sometimes their proprietors may change from year to year, but they're always fun. A shopping guide with a map as well as the self-guided walking-tour brochure of Southport's historic sites is available at the visitors center, called Southport 2000, 210 East Moore Street. The center is open weekdays from 10:00 A.M. to 5:00 P.M., sometimes open on Saturdays the same hours, and is closed Sundays. Phone (910) 457-7927.

If you decide to spend a night in Southport, the **India Oak**

Inn is an 1886 Victorian home with a full measure of ginger-bread trim, great porches with swings and rockers, and mixed period furnishings inside. The inn has two rooms with private bath and a luxury suite. In addition to a generous full breakfast, the proprietors serve chocolate-chip cookies and decaf in the evening. Rates begin at about $95 per room. Phone (910) 457–0209.

North of Southport via State Highway 133, **Brunswick Town State Historic Site** marks the first settlement in the Cape Fear area. Here you can study the remains of the colonial port town of Brunswick and the earth mounts of Fort Anderson that the Confederate Army built about 100 years later. Some of the old foundations have been excavated and are uncovered as archaeological exhibits. The mounds have survived pretty much intact since the Civil War and actually make a good spot from which to see the older ruins. A visitors center on the site has slide presentations and exhibits about the colonial town and the artifacts excavated from the ruins. This is one of those well-managed sites where you can learn about both colonial life and the Civil War, and get a sense of the continuity from the one time to the other. Brunswick Town is open April 1 through October 31, Monday through Saturday from 9:00 A.M. to 5:00 P.M., from Sunday 1:00 to 5:00 P.M. November 1 through March 31 the site is closed Monday and hours are shortened to 10:00 A.M. to 4:00 P.M. Tuesday through Saturday and from 1:00 to 4:00 P.M., Sunday. These hours may vary, so it's a good idea to call ahead (910) 371–6613. Admission is free.

About 10 miles north of Southport, still on Highway 133, you come to **Orton Plantation Gardens**, a delight for anyone who loves flowers and grand old trees. The first owners were James and Luola Sprunk, who built terraces and ornamental gardens with live oaks lining the walkways. Later, with the help of a landscape architect, additional gardens and water features were added, and the gardens were opened to the public. Blooms extend over a long season, beginning with camellias in late winter; azaleas in spring; oleander, crepe myrtle, and magnolias in summer and fall. Plantings of annuals add extra splashes of color. Orton House, a good example of Southern antebellum architecture, is an impressive feature on the property too, but it is a private residence, so you must content yourself with admiring the exterior and visiting the small family chapel that is open to the public.

The gardens are open daily March through August from 8:00 A.M. to 6:00 P.M., September and November from 8:00 A.M. to 5:00 P.M. Admission is $7.00 for adults, $3.00 for children. Phone (910) 371–6851.

After this, the easiest thing to do is return to Highway 17 to drive on up to **Wilmington.** People who live here call Wilmington the best kept secret in North Carolina. They're of two minds as to whether that's good or bad. The thriving, historic community has a full share of entrepreneurial types who've done much to revitalize waterfront areas and old downtown buildings. They welcome tourists and new business. Some of the old-timers would rather the community's cultural and historical attractions not become too well known, lest all the new traffic spoil the ambience.

In 1989, Wilmington, which was settled before the Revolutionary War and during the Civil War was the last Atlantic port open to blockade runners, celebrated its 250th anniversary.

Historic restoration and preservation in the official ✦**Historic Wilmington District** have produced an appealing neighborhood that deserves more attention. One interesting approach is the **Wilmington Adventure Walking Tour,** by Bob Jenkins (910–763–1785). The tour takes about two hours. Jenkins calls it a "casual stroll on the original survey of the 1734 city." It takes in town houses, gardens, commercial buildings, churches, and fountains. The tour concludes with an 1858 theater and an 1892 courthouse and includes a twelve-minute video showing more sightseeing possibilities in the entire Cape Fear region. Tours run from April 1 through October. They leave daily at 10:00 A.M. and 2:00 P.M. from the foot of Market Street on the Cape Fear River. Look for a guide with a straw hat and a walking stick. Reservations are not necessary. Tickets are $10.00 for adults, $5.00 for children ages six to twelve.

There are two buildings in the area worth seeing inside. The beautifully restored **1770 Burgin–Wright House** (910–762–0570) stands at the corner of Third and Market streets. It was built in 1770 on the foundation of the abandoned Wilmington City Jail. One reason the owner chose this site and kept the foundation was because it had a tunnel running down to the water, so he could get to the boats without going outside. Tours are offered Tuesday through Saturday at 10:20 and 11:20 A.M. and 1:20, 2:20, and 3:20 P.M. Admission is $3.00 for adults, $1.00 for full-time

10

students. The **Zebulon Latimer House** (910– 762–0492) at 126 South Third Street is one of the few remaining examples of a town house of the time. The same family inhabited it from its completion in 1852 until the historical society took it over in the 1960s. About 60 percent of the furnishings are the family's original belongings. Three of the four floors are open, so you can see everything from beds to china. The house also has archives and a library for those who want to study further, with a researcher available on Tuesdays and Thursdays. The house is open Tuesday through Saturday from 10:00 A.M. to 4:00 P.M. If a tour is in process when you arrive, you may join it, or be taken separately by a docent, or wait for the next group to gather. Admission is $3.00 for adults, $1.00 for full-time students.

Another pleasant way to see the Wilmington District is to take a **Springbrook Farms** sight-seeing tour (910–251–8889) by horse-drawn carriage, with a driver who narrates as you pass the historic sites. At Christmas a nice touch is that you ride in a closed reindeer-drawn carriage, snuggled in a lap rug, for a tour narrated by Santa. Owner–operator John Pucci says this appeals especially to children and romantics. Tours leave from the corner of Water and Market streets. They run from 10:00 A.M. to 10:00 P.M. Tuesday through Sunday, from April through October. During November, December, and March, tours run from 7:00 to 10:00 P.M. Friday, 11:00 A.M. to 10:00 P.M. Saturday, and 11:00 A.M. to 4:00 P.M. Sunday. These hours may vary. Sometimes tours may be arranged for different times by appointment. Rates are $8.00 for adults, $4.00 for children.

One attraction that definitely deserves more attention is ◆ **St. John's Museum of Art,** at 114 Orange Street (910–763–0281). The museum, which is tastefully light and airy, comprises three historic buildings: a Masonic Lodge (1804), the Cowan House Studio (ca. 1830), and what was St. Nicholas Greek Orthodox Church (1943). A sculpture garden ties the complex together. The permanent collection features 200 years of North Carolinian art. The most important gift the museum has received is the original color prints of Mary Cassatt, the nineteenth-century American artist who worked with the Impressionists in France. The museum also has a dozen temporary exhibitions that change annually. Open Tuesday through Saturday from 10:00 A.M. to 5:00 P.M. and Sunday from noon to 4:00 P.M. Admission is $2.00 for adults, $1.00 for children under age eighteen, $5.00 for families; children age five and under are free. Admission the first Sunday of every month is free.

From the inn, you can walk to ◆ **Chandler's Wharf,** on the Cape Fear River, a complex of restored historical warehouses and buildings with cobblestone streets, picket fences, and pretty streams. Instead of maritime businesses, the buildings now hold specialty shops and restaurants. **The Riverboat Landing Restaurant** (910–763–7227) is operated by an Italian family but offers many more seafood specialties than pasta dishes. It's a casual place where you're at ease in either dressy or casual clothes, and even fussy kids do OK here because while you're enjoying fresh grouper or cioppino, they can have spaghetti or lasagna. And even though the proprietors are playing down their Italian offerings to promote their seafood (they say, "Remember,

The Battleship *USS North Carolina*

Italians are fishermen, too"), they make a wicked cannoli that no one should miss. Beer, wine, and mixed drinks are available in the lounge and dining room. In good weather, some of the nicest dining areas are those on outdoor and glass-enclosed balconies overlooking the river. Prices are moderate. Open for lunch and dinner. Hours vary seasonally; call for exact times.

Also in Chandler's Wharf, **Elizah's Oyster Bar,** on the waterfront, is open from 11:30 A.M. to midnight, Tuesday through Saturday. The place is known for its hot crab dip and good house wines.

Another complex of eight restored old buildings, the ◆ **Cotton Exchange** (910–343–9896), beginning on Front Street between Walnut and Grace, features almost thirty shops and restaurants, including Paddy's Hollow, a Victorian pub, and East Bank Trading Company, a shop of American handcrafts. Most of the shops are open from 10:00 A.M. to 5:00 P.M. Monday through Saturday and from 1:00 to 5:00 P.M. Sunday. The restaurants are open evenings as well.

From all these points along the river, you can see the ◆ **USS North Carolina Battleship Memorial,** commissioned in 1941 and considered the world's greatest battleship at the time. The ship has been docked as a memorial since 1961. The self-guided tour, which takes about two hours, leads you through the crew's quarters, galley, sick bay, engine room, and pilothouse. What you see is fascinating in its technical detail. If you're the kind of person who embarrasses genteel guides in historic homes by asking what they used for toilet paper, this tour is definitely for you. A short orientation film starts you off.

A more glitzy approach to the same ship is the outdoor sound and light show, "The Immortal Showboat," offered every night at 9:00 P.M. from the first Friday in June through Labor Day. The audience sits in a 1,000-seat grandstand across from the ship's port bow, while voices, lights, music, and special-effect ordnance fire dramatize the ship's history for seventy minutes. The ship looms out of the water where Highways 17, 74, 76, and 421 intersect, 3 miles outside Wilmington. In addition to a good-sized parking lot, you'll find a center for visitors with a gift shop, snack bar, and picnic shelter. The ship (910–251–5797) is open every day from 8:00 A.M. to sunset. Write USS *North Carolina* Battleship Memorial, P.O. Box 417, Wilmington 28402. Admission is $6.00 for adults, $3.00 for children.

During the summer an alternative to parking at the battleship site is to take the **Riverboat Taxi** over from Chandler's Wharf. Originally it was a World War II U.S. Navy launch. It leaves every half hour for the battleship from 10:00 A.M. to 5:00 P.M. daily. Modest rates.

You can't get seasick on the battleship unless you have a wildly vivid imagination, and the launch ride is too short to do much damage. If you'd like to test your sea legs a bit more realistically, you could try a riverboat cruise on the ◆ *Henrietta II,* which docks at the foot of Market Street on the Cape Fear River. These cruises are party affairs, ranging from Sunday sight-seeing cruises to evening Dogwood cruises in spring, a sweetheart cruise on Valentine's Day, and weekend dinner cruises. It's all planned and public, but if you're in the mood for it, the gaiety can be a lot of fun. The original *Henrietta* was the first steam paddleboat built in North Carolina, and it ran the river between Wilmington and Fayetteville for forty years. James Seawell (no joke), the builder, named it for his daughter. The *Henrietta II* is a nearly new paddleboat and includes a dance floor and an air-conditioned dining room, in addition to the outdoor deck space you'd expect. If she can see this modern version, poor Henrietta is probably wishing herself back to the future.

LAND OF FERRIES AND FORTS

Just a few miles away from the historic port of Wilmington you come to a series of beaches: Wrightsville, Carolina, Wilmington, and Kure. The entire area has more historic sites and interesting spots to visit than can be included in a book covering the entire state. For folks seeking out-of-the-way places, the beaches don't offer the same secluded charm as the Brunswick Islands, but they can be fun, with enough amusement and entertainment to please the kids without doing in Mom and Dad, especially if you avoid the peak summer season. A number of historical and marine attractions are especially important and interesting.

◆ **Wrightsville Beach** is 12 miles east of Wilmington. It operates as a year-round island resort and has plenty of motels and some nice, casual, moderately priced seafood restaurants.

Driving south from Wilmington on Highway 421 for a little less than 20 miles takes you to the beaches on **Pleasure Island.** All this area is highly commercial and built up, but if you stick it out to Kure Beach, you'll find two attractions worth taking time to see if you're interested in the naval aspects of Civil War history and in marine life.

Three miles south of Kure Beach, on Highway 421, is ◆ **Fort Fisher National Historic Site.** The fort stood up under heavy naval attack during the Civil War, and some of the 25-foot earthwork fortifications that protected the Cape Fear River and the port of Wilmington from Union forces remain. Reading about such parapets is one thing; looking at them and musing on how they must have been built before the days of bulldozers is a more vivid experience, intensified by such touches as a reconstruction of the gun emplacement and a history trail. There's also a museum that displays Civil War artifacts and offers a slide show on the history of the fort. If you travel with a picnic cooler, you'll enjoy the picnic area on the site. Admission is free but donations are appreciated (910–458–5538). Open April through October, 9:00 A.M. to 5:00 P.M., Monday through Saturday, 1:00 to 5:00 P.M. Sunday; November through March 10, 10:00 A.M. to 4:00 P.M. Tuesday through Saturday, 1:00 to 4:00 P.M. Sunday, and closed Monday and major holidays.

Across from Fort Fisher National Historic Site, the ◆ **North Carolina Aquarium** features a 20,000-gallon shark aquarium, a whale exhibit, and a touch tank where children (and adults too, for that matter) can actually handle some kinds of marine life. There are also *koi* (carp) pools and river otters. The aquarium maintains a full schedule of special events and educational programs. It might be worth calling ahead for a schedule (910–458–8257). Admission is free. Open from 9:00 A.M. to 5:00 P.M. Monday through Saturday, and from 1:00 to 5:00 P.M. Sunday. Closed Thanksgiving, Christmas, and New Year's Day.

When you get this far south on the island, you will have two choices. You can take the Fort Fisher Ferry to Southport, which brings you close to the Brunswick Islands, whence you began driving, or you can backtrack up the island and take the bridge across to Wilmington, also whence you began driving. At first glance, the obvious way to avoid those whences and the dilemma of decision would be to begin by taking the ferry from Southport to Fort Fisher, then drive north on the island and finally cross over to the delights of Wilmington. You may indeed decide to do it that way, especially if you're not traveling during the peak summer months. But you need to know that the ferry leaves

15

Southport only seven times a day; crossing takes an hour; it accommodates only twenty automobiles at a time; and the time schedule may change. Trying to learn and meet a schedule, only to end up waiting in a line that has–cut off several cars ahead of you because the ferry is already full, is not the stuff relaxing vacations are made of. For more current information when you decide, phone (919) 458–3329. Some information is also available from the Cape Fear Coast Convention and Visitors Bureau (800–222–4757 in the eastern United States, 800–922–7117 in North Carolina, or 910–341–4030).

Should you decide to backtrack to Wilmington, you can give the kids a pleasant break by stopping at the ◆ **Tote-em-in Zoo,** about 10 miles south of Wilmington on Highway 421. The zoo, which has been in business more than thirty-five years, features more than 100 different animals, a museum of exotic mounted specimens, and another museum of varied artifacts from around the world, including arrowheads and World War II items. Modest rates. Open from spring thaw until the first hard freeze, roughly March through November, from 9:00 A.M. to 5:00 P.M. weekdays and until 6:30 P.M. weekends. Call ahead because hours vary seasonally and according to weather (910–791–0472).

If you're interested in North Carolina wineries, you may want to schedule a side trip while you're in the Wilmington area to ◆ **Duplin Wine Cellars,** about an hour's drive from the coast. The winery is in Rose High, on Highway 117, about halfway between Wilmington and Goldsboro. The winery conducts tours and tastings and, of course, sells the wines. Tours are preceded by an audiovisual presentation on the history of southern winemaking. Duplin Wine Cellars (910–289–3888) is especially well known for its Magnolia, a soft dry table wine, and its scuppernong dessert wine. The word *scuppernong* is an Indian word meaning "sweet tree."

Scuppernong is the oldest grape in America, and the Duplin Cellars is the only winery in America that makes 100 percent scuppernong wine. Open Monday through Saturday, from 9:00 A.M. to 5:00 P.M. Closed New Year's Day, July 4, Labor Day, Thanksgiving Day, and Christmas Day. Write for a free newsletter: P.O. Box 756, Rose Hill 28458.

From Wilmington, the best way to head north is to drive on Highway 17 for a while. Stretches of it are annoyingly full of strip-city areas where traffic is heavy and slow. Taking some of the little side roads seems like a good idea, and you can if you wish without fear of getting lost, because most of them eventually loop back to Highway 17 anyway. But the loops are disappointing. You won't find much but scrubland, little clusters of homes or mobile homes, and perhaps some tobacco fields. It's OK for a break but quickly becomes about as boring as the more direct approach on Highway 17.

One interesting stop, right on the highway shortly after you leave Wilmington, is the ◆ **Poplar Grove Plantation.** It has an unusual history in that it not only survived the Civil War, but it also became economically successful again by growing peanuts. The original plantation operated in the tradition of the times, as a self-supporting agricultural community with more than sixty slaves. The manor house burned down in 1849 and was rebuilt the following year where it now stands. When you visit the plantation, guides in period costume lead you on a tour of the manor house—a three-floor Greek Revival building—and the outbuildings, describing what daily life on the plantation was like.

Now that the plantation's restaurant, which serves lunch and dinner, has been moved from the manor house into a new building built just for the restaurant (call 910–686–9503 for current hours, menus, and prices), the size and variety of exhibits in the manor house have been increased to make a complete plantation museum. The top floor displays bedrooms. On the main floor a parlor, dining room, and library are filled with appropriate period pieces. On the lower floor you'll find displays of handmade textiles, old quilts and coverlets, a floor loom, spinning wheels, and other textile-related artifacts such as an early Singer sewing machine, a clock reel, and a mother-in-law. The mother-in-law isn't going to ask to go home with you or anything; it's a device for winding yarn without an extra person to hold it.

In another room a series of displays depict agricultural activities from 1860 to 1960, especially peanut production. This was a peanut plantation, remember. The equipment includes a horse-drawn peanut planter and an assortment of hand tools, many found buried on the site. Photographs add detail to the exhibit.

When you visit you'll probably have an opportunity to watch some crafts demonstrations. The plantation has three resident craftspeople: a blacksmith, a weaver, and a basket maker. At least one of them, and often two, is always demonstrating. Some of what they make, rag rugs for instance, is for sale.

The outbuildings include a tenant house, smokehouse, herb cellar, kitchen (plantation kitchens were always in separate buildings), blacksmith shop, and turpentine and saltworks display. With or without a guide, looking at these buildings dramatically brings home some realities of history. A visitor looking at the small, roughly finished, uninsulated tenant house said, "It's hard to imagine that a whole family actually lived in here." Another visitor, seeing the mock hams, sausages, and bacons hanging in the smokehouse, wondered what the real thing would have been like in such hot weather and said, "It's a wonder everybody didn't die of food poisoning."

For children, Poplar Grove Plantation has lots of open spaces, shaded with live oaks, sycamores, and magnolias, for running; a playground; and some farm animals they can see and maybe even touch.

Continuing north on Highway 17 takes you through some very local, untouristy areas, such as Holly Ridge, where the mayor's office is also the office of Ocean Aire Realty. If you want more of a sense of the area, shortly after you pass Holly Ridge turn left on Verona Road, and following the signs, head toward Haws Run. You'll go by some pretty little houses with lovingly tended gardens, then an abandoned trailer park, and finally many occupied mobile homes on the way back out to Highway 17. This detour of only a few miles gives a view of what many small North Carolina communities near the coast are like.

Then you're into the area around Jacksonville, which is shaped and colored by ✥ **Camp Lejeune Marine Base.** Traffic is fairly heavy, and the area bulges with the kind of commercial development that surrounds military bases: motels, restaurants, amusements, shopping centers, and the like. But even though driving through such a section isn't as relaxing as spinning along a country road, it's tremendously instructive and sometimes funny. Most of the people you see in most of the vehicles are heartbreakingly young men with habitually perfect posture and haircuts so short you can almost see their scalps from the next automobile. Often they're in pairs or groups, and often they're towing boats or hauling bikes. The progression of the establishments and signs they pass along the road tells a story: Foxy Lady, New Ink Tattoo Shop, Luigi's (where you can get a remarkably good Italian meal), a motel sign WELCOME MR. NUNNERY, Real

Value Diamond Outlet, an assortment of churches, and The Maternity and Newborn Store.

Here's information of a more dignified nature. Camp Lejeune is one of the most complete training centers in the world and covers 110,000 acres. You may wish to stop at the Beirut Memorial, honoring those killed in Beirut and Grenada. It is outside the gate of Camp Johnson on Highway 24. You can't get onto the base without a pass, and you can't get a pass without a driver's license and registration certificate. The information center at the main gate on Highway 24 is open twenty-four hours a day (910–451–2197).

From Jacksonville, you could logically continue up Highway 17 to New Bern, or you could travel east on Highway 24 toward the ocean to check out the Bogue Banks and then go on to Morehead City, Beaufort, and Atlantic, and ferry across to the Outer Banks. Better yet, if you're not hurrying, avoid this section of Highway 24, which runs along another edge of the Marine base, and continue north about 15 miles more on Highway 17, where you pick up Highway 58, which runs southeast along the side of the Croatan National Forest and is a much more pleasant drive to the coast. ❖ **Cedar Point** is a nice place to stop for a picnic or a rest and perhaps a hike along the Cedar Point Tideland Trail. You'll find camping areas and picnic tables in the shade along the water. Nearby is Cape Carteret, a little town that's probably completely solved its crime problem by locating its ABC (liquor) store right next to the police and town hall offices.

Aside from learning that Emerald Island is a sea turtle sanctuary, you're probably not going to find much that pleases you driving over to the Bogue Banks. The entire barrier island, which is nearly 30 miles long, has been developed commercially to the point that condos, cottages, and water slides line the beaches, and beach shops crowd one another along the highway. You may prefer to skip the Bogue Banks, stay on the mainland, and head for Beaufort.

THE NORTHERN COAST AND ISLANDS

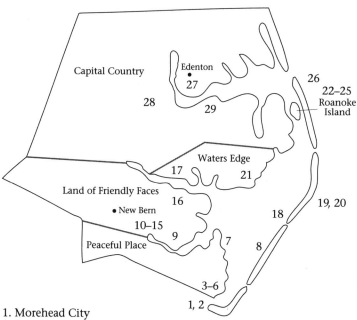

Capital Country

Edenton
• 27

28

29

26

22–25
Roanoke
Island

Waters Edge

17

21

Land of Friendly Faces

16

19, 20

• New Bern

18

10–15

9

7

Peaceful Place

8

3–6

1, 2

1. Morehead City
2. Bogue's Pocket Cafe
3. Beaufort
4. North Carolina Maritime
   Museum
5. Beaufort Historic Site Tours
6. Langdon House
7. Morris Marina
8. Portsmouth Island
9. Oriental
10. New Bern
11. Tryon Palace
12. Harmony House Inn
13. Henderson House
14. Fireman's Museum
15. Bank of the Arts
16. Aurora Fossil Museum
17. Bath

18. Ocracoke
19. Oscar's House
20. The Back Porch
21. Mattamuskeet National
    Wildlife Refuge
22. Fort Raleigh National Historic
    Site
23. *Elizabeth II* State Historic Site
24. Tranquil House Inn
25. Fisherman's Wharf
    Restaurant
26. Wright Brothers National
    Memorial
27. The Lords Proprietor's Inn
28. Hope Plantation
29. Somerset Place

THE NORTHERN COAST AND ISLANDS

PEACEFUL PLACES

Your next major stop as you head north along the coast is ❖**Morehead City,** a deep port where the Intracoastal Waterway joins the Atlantic Ocean. It is both a commercial fishing town and a summer resort area, appealing especially to sport fishers. The waterfront is more devoted to commerce than tourism, has more than 5,000 square feet of continuous wharf, and includes a lot of shipping storage space. That means the waterfront isn't really pretty; it's too commercial and busy, but the activity is authentic and interesting. As a traveler, if you aren't here to fish, you're probably here to eat fish. The area has plenty of moderately priced motels and more seafood restaurants than you could patronize in two weeks' hard eating. If you ask people where to go, they'll most often make the unlikely sounding recommendation of the **Sanitary Fish Market Restaurant** (919– 247–3111). It's just a block from Highway 70, on Bogue Sound. This is a big, casual, family-oriented place that seats more than 600 people and serves all kinds of seafood and no alcohol. It has been owned and operated by the same family for more than fifty years. Open from 11:00 A.M. to 9:00 P.M. daily. Closed in December.

If you say you don't want to go where everybody goes but want to eat at a place only a special few know about, you'll probably end up at the ❖**Bogue's Pocket Cafe.** The proprietors of this newish restaurant, at 715 Evans Street, are Caroline Robinson and Martha Bourne. Martha sums up the difference between the Bogue's Pocket Cafe and the majority of other local seafood restaurants metaphorically, "We don't serve hush puppies." Also, the place is comparatively small, seating about sixty people at most. The menu changes weekly, depending on what is available at the docks for its inspiration. "What we prepare is always fresh and local," Martha says. She prefers grilling, baking, and sautéing to deep-frying. The bread and desserts are homemade. One of the most popular desserts recently has been the chocolate Grand Marnier cake, the kind of dessert you might as well just pat directly onto your hips. Beer and wine are available. Dress is casual. Given the restaurant's exterior, it almost has to be. Can you seriously picture dressing to the teeth to go into a green cinder-block building with purple stripes? As an innkeeper in

Beaufort who often sends guests to the Bogue's Pocket Cafe said, "It's strange to look at, but the food is out of this world." In the summer the restaurant is open daily from 11:00 A.M. to 2:00 P.M. for lunch and from 6:00 to 10:00 P.M. for dinner. In the off-season the restaurant is open the same hours Tuesday through Saturday. Reservations are not accepted. Occasionally during slow times, the proprietors will close to take a week off, so if you're traveling in the off-season, it's a good idea to call ahead (919–247–5351).

From Morehead City it's just a short drive over the Paul Graydon Bridge to ◆ **Beaufort.** The first step to having fun in Beaufort is learning to say it properly—*Bow'-ford.* This separates it from that place in South Carolina spelled the same way but pronounced to rhyme with "phew." People in Beaufort, North Carolina, care and repond accordingly.

This was once a fishing village, settled by French Huguenots and English sailors more than 275 years ago. The port was active during three wars: the American Revolution, the War of 1812, and the Civil War. Today, Beaufort is a laid-back vacation area in which historic preservation and restoration have been impressive. Much of the downtown has been designated a National Historic Landmark, and the Beaufort Historical Association has restored a number of early buildings that are open to the public.

Local art is offered in the **Mattie King Davis Art Gallery** on the grounds of the Old Town Beaufort Restoration Complex, where local artists and craftspeople display their pottery, weaving, oil painting, watercolors, and other original art. It's open April 1 through October, Monday through Saturday from 10:00 A.M. to 4:00 P.M. No admission fee.

The ◆ **North Carolina Maritime Museum,** 315 Front Street, contains artifacts ranging from fish and fossils to ships, including a model-ship collection and a collection of 5,000 seashells from all over the world. Open Monday through Friday from 9:00 A.M. to 5:00 P.M., Saturday from 10:00 A.M. to 5:00 P.M., Sunday from 1:00 P.M. to 5:00 P.M. (919) 728–7317. For a schedule of special events, write the museum at 315 Front Street, Beaufort 28516.

One way to see the sights and learn a lot about local lore is by taking one of the ◆ **Beaufort Historic Site Tours** operated by the historical association. All tours leave from the 1825 Josiah Bell House where the welcome center is located. Call ahead for all tour arrangements, (919) 728–5225, Monday through Saturday from 8:30 A.M. to 4:30 P.M.

The home tour includes not only old homes, but also the jail, courthouse, and apothecary shop. Tours run Monday through Saturday from 9:30 A.M. to 3:30 P.M. Admission is $5.00 for adults, $2.00 for children. A ten percent discount for groups of thirty or more is offered.

From April 11 through October, the narrated English double-decker bus tours cover the downtown district and go out past a house that is reputed to have been a hangout for Blackbeard and his pirates in the late 1600s. The tour narrator gives a lively mix of fact and folklore. These tours run Wednesdays and Saturdays at 11:00 A.M. and cost $5.00 per seat. Special charters for up to fifty-six people cost $200. Charter rate for school groups is $100.

If you can get together a group of at least six people, you can book a narrated tour of the Old Burying Ground at Ann Street, where stones date back to 1709 and possibly earlier. The narrator tells colorful stories about unusual circumstances through which people came to be buried here. Admission is $3.00 for adults, $2.00 for children. You may walk around the grounds anytime free.

Of the several bed-and-breakfast establishments you might choose, ◆**Langdon House,** at 123 Craven Street (919–728–5499), is especially congenial. This colonial home, built in 1732, is the oldest building in Beaufort operated as a bed and breakfast. All four rooms have private baths and queen-size beds. Two porches, one on the first and another on the second floor, invite people watching, stargazing, and woolgathering. Breakfast is a full show—no soggy doughnuts in a box with coffee in Styrofoam cups here. Some mornings, for instance, it's orange pecan waffles with orange butter.

Part of the establishment's charm comes from the antiques, including paintings and musical instruments that earlier residents of the building have donated in the interests of the restoration's authenticity. A bigger attraction yet is the congeniality of the people. Jimm Prest knows the area intimately and likes to talk about it.

Langdon House is a small operation. Jimm and a little extra help usually run the show, which means personal attention that is pretty much one-on-one with guests. Want to sleep till noon and have breakfast late? Jimm's willing. He says he wishes more people understood that if you want that kind of small-town, individualized situation, you can't expect chain-motel desk service at the same time. You may call for a reservation, for instance, and get a message on the answering machine saying that Jimm's gone for groceries or a haircut, or a couple days' vacation, telling you when he'll return, and asking you to call back then, as you'd do if you were phoning a friend.

Having been in the area so long, Jimm is especially well qualified to suggest eating places. He often recommends the previously described Bogue's Pocket Cafe in Morehead City. But for people who don't want to get back in the car after settling in, he suggests the **Net House,** a short walk away on Turner Street, where you can get broiled or lightly battered and fried seafood. You'll recognize it when you get to it because it has a big red crab in front.

Langdon House cooperates in handling overflow and referring extra guests with the **Captain's Quarters,** a bed and breakfast in a Victorian house at 315 Ann Street (919–728–7711). Captain Dick and Ruby Collins like to chat. Captain Dick's title comes not from the sea, as you might suppose, but from his days as an airline pilot. When you appear for your continental breakfast, he says, "Top o' the mornin' to ya!"

One could stay in Beaufort a long time just wandering around, eating seafood, and sitting on the porch reading trashy novels. Assuming you want to see more, however, you should push on north almost to the end of Highway 70 East, to the little town of **Atlantic** (not to be confused with Atlantic Beach), where you can catch the ferry to the Outer Banks. Actually, you can't catch it; you're going to have to call ahead and arrange this part of your trip carefully. At ✦**Morris Marina,** Don and Katie Morris run their private ferry business taking sightseers and fishers to various sites along the islands of Outer Banks. Don can tell stories of these places for about as long as you want to listen.

In particular, visit ✦**Portsmouth Island.** It's uninhabited now, but 635 people once lived on the 30-mile-long island in the village of Portsmouth. Ultimately, they couldn't survive the weather, especially hurricanes. A particularly bad one in 1846 opened Hatteras and Oregon inlets and changed shipping patterns, which cut off future economic development for the village. Gradually, the people left, first the young and then the old. According to Joel Arrington, writing in the magazine *Wildlife in North Carolina,* only fourteen people remained on the island in 1950; the last male resident died in 1971, after which the remaining two women gave up and moved to the mainland. The buildings of the village remain a little beat-up but intact, maintained by the U.S. Park Service.

Your difficulty in seeing the village will be that even after you've ferried across to the island, you need a four-wheel-drive vehicle to travel the 18 miles up the beach from the ferry landing to get to the village, because there are no roads. But getting a ride in a four-wheel-drive vehicle in North Carolina isn't as hard as it sounds. They are ubiquitous, especially among sportsmen (and it's not sexist to leave out women here, for there are few). Enough such people like to visit the village that by planning ahead with Don Morris you should be able to arrange a ride if you don't have a four-wheeler of your own. Indeed, the sight of half a dozen or so men in fishing clothes, sitting quietly on the benches inside the old, weathered, and abandoned Portsmouth Village Methodist Church when they're supposed to be at water's edge fishing, may be as special an experience as visiting the village. This isn't a likely place to lodge. A few cabins, locally known as "hooches," are rented, but during peak fishing seasons they're reserved as much as two years ahead of time. Still, if you'd like to try some truly primitive conditions on the island, it doesn't hurt to ask. For information about ferry hours and renting hooches, write Morris Marina at Star Route Box 761, Atlantic 28511, or phone (919) 225–4261.

A simpler way to visit the village, though less colorful and a bit more *on* the beaten (or should it be *rowed,* in this case?) path, is to take a skiff from Ocracoke Island that brings you directly to the spot. You need to arrange in advance. Phone Rudi Austin (919–928–4361) or Judas Austin (919–928–4281) to charter a ferry. The more people you can round up to make the trip with you, the less it costs per person. Figure about $40 for two, round-trip, but only about $15 per person when you have three or more.

If you're not sure how to manage the trip and would like more information and advice, call the Ranger Station (919–728–2250) for enthusiastic, knowledgeable help.

LAND OF FRIENDLY FACES

The entire area along the northern coast, the barrier islands, and the Outer Banks is a maze of toll ferries, free ferries, private ferries, and bridges. The way you organize your trips here depends on everything from the weather to how much time you want to spend driving or being ferried. Remember that a ferry is not a fast way to travel. In planning trips in this area, sometimes it works better to find a pleasant base to which you return after each foray in a new direction. Try New Bern as a slightly inland base from which, one way or another, you can get to a wonderful variety of places to spend a day or so. Everyone in New Bern will have ideas for you, which will certainly include ❖ **Oriental.**

Oriental is about 25 miles east of New Bern on Highway 55. It has won a reputation as the sailing capital of the East Coast and almost always has a sailing school or camp in process. Except for a couple of antiques shops, a modest motel or two, and some simple restaurants, there's not much here except nice people. If you want to spend a night at a bed and breakfast here, the **Tar Heel Inn** in Oriental at 205 Church Street (919–249–1078) has six rooms with private baths, king- and queen-size beds, and handicap facilities. The inn was built at the turn of the century and has been restored to duplicate the feel of an English country inn—with contemporary amenities. The innkeepers, Dave and Patti Nelson, serve a big breakfast.

Then again, once you're in ❖ **New Bern** you may not want to go anywhere else at all, not just because there's so much to see and do but also because this is one of the friendliest towns anywhere. To give you an idea, a couple staying at a bed-and-breakfast inn in the historic district was walking to a nearby restaurant where they had dinner reservations when they stopped to admire an especially nicely restored house. The owners, who happened to be on the porch, invited the couple in for a drink and showed them around. They spent so much time chatting that the couple never did make it to the restaurant.

On the outside chance that you might not be so generously befriended by strangers, stop in the tourist center at the Chamber of Commerce about 2 blocks from Highway 70, near the Trent River at the end of Middle Street, when you get to town. Signs point the way from all major entrances. Everyone here is extraordinarily friendly, too. One middle-aged travel writer who stopped in for maps and directions struck up a conversation with a teenage summer assistant. They've been corresponding ever since.

If you're an antiquer, be sure to get a copy of the brochure "Antiques Shops of New Bern," which gives particulars on more than a dozen antiques shops, complete with a map and an explanation of American furniture styles from Queen Anne (1725–1750) through the arts and crafts and mission styles of the early 1900s.

You'll also be able to pick up full details on ◆ **Tryon Palace** Restorations and Garden Complex, where first a royal government and then an independent state government were housed. In colonial times Tryon Palace was known as the most beautiful building in America. The elaborate formal gardens as well as the elegant buildings and furnishings have been restored.

Tours conducted by guides in costume lead you through the rooms; give you a look at demonstrations of candle making, cloth making, cooking, and other period activities; and fill you in on specific facts about the buildings and their earlier, illustrious occupants. If you just want to walk around in the gardens, you can take a self-guided tour. The complex (919–514–4900 or 800–767–1560) is open year-round, Monday through Saturday

Tryon Palace, New Bern

28

from 9:30 A.M. to 4:00 P.M., and Sunday from 1:30 to 4:00 P.M. Closed Thanksgiving Day, December 24–26, and January 1. Admission is $12.00 for adults, $6.00 for students with identification. Write Tryon Palace, Box 1007, New Bern 28560.

An interesting and historical, yet cheery and comfortable place to stay in New Bern is ◆ **Harmony House Inn,** 215 Pollock Street (919–636–3810). Sooki and Ed Kirkpatrick, the proprietors, bring to innkeeping the kind of personable warmth that makes business travelers who stay there regularly feel free to stop in unannounced, use the phone in the inn's office, and then hurry out to the car, saying they'll be back to spend the night on the way through tomorrow.

The story of the house is complex. The house began as a four-room, two-story home with Greek Revival styling. As the family grew, the house was enlarged; then around the turn of the century, as the children grew older, two sons wanted the house, so it was sawed in half, and one side was moved 9 feet away from the other. A huge hallway and another set of stairs were put in to join the building yet divide it into two separate dwellings. Now the two hallways, front doors, and sitting areas are all part of the inn. It's furnished with antiques, reproductions created by local craftspeople, and in the parlor is an 1875 organ in perfect working order. Breakfast is always an extravaganza, including eggs, cheese, meat, cereal, and fruit. You are invited to participate in an evening social hour with white wine, and later sherry is put out in case you'd like a nightcap.

After a day of touring, you can rest awhile at the Harmony House Inn and then walk to dinner. ◆ **Henderson House,** right across the street at 216 Pollock (919–637–4784), has been serving fine meals for nearly twenty years. The atmosphere is elegant. Guests are invited to tour an art gallery on the second floor where the paintings of Robert Weaver, an internationally known artist and the chef's father, are displayed. Dining specialties include southern peanut soup and cold apricot soup, as well as a seafood casserole, scallops, lobster, lamb, veal, and chicken entrees. For lunch Henderson House offers such delights as broiled crabmeat on English muffin and Fruits de Mer en Croute. All spirits are available. As you'd expect, all the desserts are homemade. Everything is delicious, the kind of dining guests at the bed and breakfasts talk about over breakfast the next morning. Also as you'd expect, the prices are not inexpensive. Lunch is served from 11:30 A.M. to 2:00 P.M., dinner from 6:00 to 9:00 P.M. Closed Sunday, Monday, and Tuesday.

On a day when you haven't put all your energy into touring the palace, you might check out three small, less well-known museums, each within walking distance of the other.

The **Attmore–Oliver House Museum,** built in 1790, at 511 Broad Street (parking at 510 Pollock Street), belonged at one time to Samuel Chapman, who had earlier been a first lieutenant under General George Washington. It features eighteenth- and nineteenth-century antiques, artifacts related to New Bern's history, and a Civil War museum room. There's also a collection of eighteenth-century dolls. Open Tuesday through Saturday from 1:00 to 4:30 P.M. (919–638–8558). Closed mid-December to the first weekend in April. Modest fee.

✦**Fireman's Museum,** across the corner at 411 Hancock Street, houses a collection of memorabilia of North Carolina's earliest fire company, from 1845, and of the Button Company, a rival volunteer company. The museum guide himself has been a volunteer fireman for many years. The displays include early steamers and pump wagons, large photographs, and the mounted head of an old fire horse named Fred, who, at least according to publicists, died in harness answering a false alarm in 1925. No information is offered about what happened to the rest of the horse. Open Tuesday through Saturday from 9:30 A.M. to noon from and 1:00 to 5:00 P.M.; Sunday from 1:00 to 5:00 P.M. Closed Thanksgiving, Christmas, and New Year's Day. Modest fee (919–636–4087).

At ✦**Bank of the Arts,** 317 Middle Street (919–638–2577), about a block away, you'll find artists' exhibits in sculpture, oil, watercolor, pottery, and photography. The exhibits change every month. Originally a neoclassical bank building, it is now home of the Craven Arts Council and Gallery. The gallery has 30-foot-high ceilings with ornate colored plaster in the Beaux Arts style. Sometimes afternoon concerts, storytellers, and folksingers are featured. Open weekdays from 10:00 A.M. to 4:00 P.M. and Saturday from 11:00 A.M. to 5:00 P.M. Closed Sunday. Admission is free.

In a town as historically significant as New Bern, you could easily get into more historical data than you really want on a vacation, but to enjoy the area you should know at least a few basic facts. The community was first settled in 1710, by Swiss and German immigrants, who named it for Bern, Switzerland. It was capital of the colonies from 1766 to 1776 and then state capital. Economically, the area flourished mostly because of its port at the time of the Revolution, slumped during the Civil War, then recovered fairly quickly. From about the time of World War II, it has restored gradually its historical spots and become a comfortably established, low-key attraction. Irrelevant but fun to know: Pepsi-Cola was invented here, but the guy went bankrupt during a sugar scarcity; and the official New Bern shrub is *Lagerstroemia*—crepe myrtle. The brilliant blossoms brighten most streets and home landscapes many months of the year.

WATER'S EDGE

One interesting trip from New Bern is the drive north on Highway 17 to Washington, where you pick up Highway 264 to Bath, Belhaven, and **Swan Quarter.** The trip winds through mostly rural areas, although just north of New Bern on Highway 17 you'll come to a business area where you can buy supplies. Stop at the **Eagle Supermarket,** which is a lot more fun and will give you a much better sense of the local population than the little convenience stores along the way. Out front everything from bales of straw to wheelbarrows is stacked along the windows. Inside are all the standard grocery store offerings plus some of the friendliest local employees you'll ever meet. The store is open from 7:00 A.M. to 9:00 P.M. Monday through Saturday and from 8:00 A.M. to 9:00 P.M. Sunday.

You'll find more local color just before you come to Washington, at **Chocowinity,** billed as "Home of the Indians," where the high school boasts having won a series of state and regional girls' basketball titles and cheerleading championships, beginning in 1980. It's all detailed proudly on a huge sign in front of the school. Around the corner on Highway 33 West, L Cheapos Flea Market and Scotts Collectibles and Antiques stand side by side, with old furniture, knickknacks, and odds and ends packed inside, jammed into the windows, and overflowing out onto the sidewalks. These aren't the kinds of places where you expect operating hours to remain unchanged month to month, but if you happen by when the establishments are open, you can have a lot of fun browsing, chatting, and maybe making an honest-to-goodness find. Chocowinity is a crossroads community, not set up to lure or serve tourists, so don't count on it as a place to stop, fuel up, eat, and so on. Look at it as an absolutely honest glimpse of small-town coastal North Carolina.

From here you can drive on through Washington to Bath or get to Bath by crossing the Pamlico River on the ferry, which you approach by following Highway 33 East from Chocowinity through corn and tobacco country, past a brick house with a stonework chimney that's bigger than the house, past Possum Track Road and on to Aurora—a drive of about 33 miles. This route actually backtracks some, and you could get to Aurora faster by taking State Road 1003 from Highway 17 just outside New Bern, but then you'd miss Chocowinity. It all depends on how much exploring you want to do.

If you're interested in fossils, especially fish fossils from the Pliocene period, be sure to take time in Aurora to visit the ◆ **Aurora Fossil Museum** on Main Street (919–322–4238). Margaret McMicken, who lives right there in town, is in charge of the museum, but she's the only employee, so if she has a doctor's appointment or wants lunch or needs to attend a tourism meeting, she closes the museum during her absence. If you're coming from a distance, be sure to call ahead. Should you get there at a time when the museum is closed, you are welcome to scavenge through the piles of rejects across the street from the museum to gather your own fossils. Usual hours are from 9:00 A.M. to 4:30 P.M., Monday through Friday, 9:00 A.M. to 2:00 P.M. Saturday, and by appointment. Admission is free.

A mile or so outside Aurora, Highway 306 North turns left, bringing you to Keith Brantley's service station, the kind of place where some of the local old-timers sit around inside and talk about the weather, where whoever pumps your gas actually cleans your windshield, and where you need a key and a good kick on the door to get into the rest room. Across the road, **Brunches Restaurant** serves mostly fast food without the franchise chain atmosphere and offers excellent iced tea. The restaurant is open from 5:30 A.M. to 8:00 P.M. daily. From there Highway 306 North goes about 7 miles to the Pamlico River Ferry, which is free; the crossing takes about twenty-five minutes. From the ferry landing, go left on Highway 92 into historic ◆ **Bath,** where you come first to the visitors center.

Bath is the kind of place you fantasize about when you dream of leaving the rat race for a simpler way of life. The town, with a population not much over 200, only 3 blocks long and 2 wide, is friendly and without guile; people cutting their grass or working in their gardens wave as you walk or drive by. They're proud of their history but see it with enough humor to name the state liquor store "Ye Olde ABC Package Store."

The folks in the **Historic Bath Visitors Center** encourage you to see the twenty-five-minute orientation film, "A Town Called Bath," before you begin a self-guided walking tour or take one of the guided tours. These begin on the hour and half hour, from 9:00 A.M. to 5:00 P.M. Monday through Saturday and from 1:00 to 5:00 P.M. Sunday, from April through October 31. Winter hours are 10:00 A.M. to 4:00 P.M. Tuesday through Saturday 1:00 to 4:00 P.M. Sunday. Tours take about an hour and a half. Modest admission charged (919–923–3971).

You can approach the history a couple of different ways. Bath was the home of Blackbeard the pirate, and some of his loot is still supposed to be buried somewhere in the area. It's also the oldest incorporated town in North Carolina. The Palmer–Marsh House, from the colonial period, dates back to about 1740. The St. Thomas Church, which was begun in 1734, is the oldest church in the state. It has been restored and is still used by the Episcopal Diocese as an active place of worship, though visitors are allowed to come in anytime for a self-guided tour. The St. Thomas parish had a collection in the early 1700s of more than 1,000 books and pamphlets from England, and that collection became the first public library in North Carolina.

While you can easily take in the tours in less than a day, if you'd like to hang around to sample the pace of Bath, you could stay at the **Bath Guest House** on South Main Street (919–923–6811). The place is operated by Paul and Irene Komarow. A 60-foot window offers a breathtaking view of the water, and in addition to a full breakfast, staying here entitles you to use the Komarows' sailboats, canoes, rowboats, and bicycles (including a bicycle built for two). Paul says he'd sell the business if someone offered him enough money—about half a million dollars—but he doesn't really expect it to happen. Still, if you've got your heart set on overnighting in Bath, call ahead and make sure that Paul, or his successor, is still there.

From Bath, it's a pretty drive of 11 miles on Highway 99 to Belhaven, where you pick up Highway 264 East, crossing the Intracoastal Waterway to Swan Quarter. Most of this distance is lovely, although you'll probably see a lot of heavy equipment in some areas. In early summer, hibiscus bushes bloom along the road, red and yellow cannas adorn the lawns of farmhouses and mobile homes, and apple trees bear so heavily that the fruit seems to be dripping from the laden and drooping branches.

At Swan Quarter you can either take the ferry to Ocracoke, probably the best known of the barrier islands, or you can continue driving up the coast along Highway 264 to Manns Harbor, where you drive across the bridge to Roanoke Island and on over the Outer Banks islands. If you plan to take the ferry, a two-and-one-half-hour ride, call the Ocracoke Visitors Center (919–928–4531) ahead of time to check on current schedules and weather conditions.

◆ **Ocracoke,** an old fishing village, is fun if you're willing to take a couple of days and just hang out; if all you do is drive through, you've missed most of what it has to offer. Of course there's history. As early as 1715, Ocracoke was a port of the North Carolina colony, where Blackbeard the pirate buried his treasure and lost his head. The head got carried off to Bath; presumably the treasure's still somewhere on the island. These days, fishing, bicycling (you can rent bicycles here), and bird hunting are bigger attractions than treasure hunting. But mostly Ocracoke is a place to escape the chrome-and-plastic world of commercial tourism. You can enjoy the remnants of Old English lilting in the speech of some of the old-timers as you walk around the village, read up on local history and nature, and visit the famous pony pens where the remaining descendants of the famous Spanish mustangs are protected. For full information about the island, ferries, and the marina, contact the Ocracoke Visitors Center (919–928–4531) or the Outer Banks Chamber of Commerce, P.O. Box 1757, Kill Devil Hills 27948 (phone 919–441–8144.)

The island has several motels and some bed-and-breakfast inns. One of the nicest is also one of the smallest. ◆ **Oscar's House** is run by Ann Ehringhaus. The name comes from Oscar, the lighthouse keeper and builder who once lived in it. The house is furnished in a style that Ann calls "comfortable and artistic." A professional photographer, she has traded some of her work with other artists, acquiring baskets, pottery, watercolors, and photographs, all of which enliven the mellow, tongue-in-groove pine walls of the house. And, as Ann says, "You can sit in the furniture. No delicate Victorian antiques."

Ann's full breakfasts feature produce from her organic garden and include everything from fresh fish to shrimp creole. It's the kind of breakfast that allows people to skip lunch. If you'd like something low-fat, vegetarian, macrobiotic, or otherwise special, Ann will accommodate you. "Cooking is my favorite part of the B&B business," she says.

A big part of the charm of staying here is getting to know Ann, who knows the island and its residents intimately. Her book, *Ocracoke Portrait,* a collection of her photographs captioned with quotations from the islanders, is an understated, elegant picture of life on the island. The inn (919–928–1311, P.O. Box 206, Ocracoke 27960) is open April through October. Special cooking workshops and photography workshops are sometimes scheduled at the beginning and end of the season. Another book to watch for is one about the complexities of innkeeping as a business and way of life. After a decade doing it, Ann is ready to write about it.

Of the several small restaurants on the island, ❖ **The Back Porch** (919–928–6401), in a shady area a half-mile north of the ferry terminal on Highway 1324, seems just right. The dining room is wood paneled, with a screened-in porch. The food is fresh, not prepared ahead, with homemade bread and desserts and subtle flavors of herb and spice that you can taste because the food isn't fried. Open daily from 5:00 to 10:00 P.M., April through November. It's good news that the restaurant now offers a cookbook of its most popular recipes.

No matter how much you like it, sooner or later you'll have to leave Ocracoke. It's possible to drive on up the Outer Banks, but it's monotonous in some undeveloped areas, full of traffic elsewhere, and generally just not as interesting as you'd expect it to be. You might do better to ferry back across to Swan Quarter and drive from there north on Highway 264, toward Manns Harbor, where the bridge takes you across to Manteo on Roanoke Island. This trip takes you into the ❖ **Mattamuskeet National Wildlife Refuge,** a breathtaking wilderness of 50,000 acres comprising Lake Mattamuskeet, marshland, timber, and cropland. The lake is 18 miles long and about 6 miles wide, the largest natural lake in North Carolina.

In parts of the acreage, water levels are controlled mechanically to allow local farmers to plant corn and soybeans and to allow for overseeding some acres to provide food for the wildlife.

The wooded areas along the boundaries of the refuge contain pine and mixed hardwoods. Some commercial logging and controlled burning are used to keep the woodlands healthy.

Headquarters for the refuge (919–926–4021) is off Highway 94, one and one-half miles north of Highway 264, between Swan Quarter and Englehard. Stopping in is a good way to learn all the possibilities of the place. At various points you can crab, fish in fresh- or saltwater, and hunt. The area begs for bird-watching, photographing, and painting. Depending on the time of year, you might spot swans, Canada geese, song- and marsh birds, and even bald eagles, as well as deer, bobcats, and river otter.

But this is a refuge administered by the U.S. Fish and Wildlife Service of the Department of the Interior and operates by its rules. You can't camp, swim, or collect exotic plants here. There are restrictions on firearms. The refuge is open from 5:00 A.M. to 9:00 P.M. daily. For full details on how to enjoy the place and lists of lodgings available nearby, write Refuge Manager, Mattamuskeet National Wildlife Refuge, Route 1, Box N-2, Swan Quarter 27885.

When you're in the area, it's fun to gas up at the **Mattamuskeet Sportsman's Center** on Highway 264, where a long-bearded proprietor and his little kids dispense information, advice, directions, and such necessities as fishing and hunting equipment, bait shrimp, worms, ice, candy, beer, and soda. Oh, yes, and food.

From Mattamuskeet Lake, Highway 264 continues through lonely marsh and woodland up to Manns Harbor and across to Roanoke Island. The main community here, Manteo, used to be a small resort area. It's growing now, not excessively, but too much to suit the longtime residents who remember when the road through town didn't turn into bumper-to-bumper ribbons of automobiles during rush hour.

ROANOKE ISLAND

You'll remember from your grade-school history lessons that Roanoke Island is where the English first tried to establish a colony in the New World in 1585, encouraged by Queen Elizabeth I and led by Sir Walter Raleigh. They named it for Raleigh but couldn't keep it going. A year later those who had survived returned to England. In 1857, Raleigh tried again, this time including women and children in the group led by John White. Virginia Dare was born here. Then Sir Walter went sailing away for supplies. By the time he got back, three years later, the colony had vanished, leaving no signs of what might have happened to it. The ◆**Fort Raleigh National Historic Site** memorializes the lost colony with a restoration of the old fort and a granite marker commemorating Virginia Dare's birth as the first English child born here. From June through August, the drama *The Lost Colony*, performed outdoors at the Waterford Theatre on the site, tells the story. One of Andy Griffith's acting roles in his pre-Mayberry years was as Sir Walter Raleigh in this show. Moderate admission charged. Phone (919) 473–3414 for exact schedules.

Next to the theater, the **Elizabethan Gardens** (919–473–3234) created by the Garden Club of North Carolina as a memorial to the lost colonists, bloom from spring until fall, with roses, crepe myrtle, lilies, hydrangeas, and summer annuals. The garden features an extensive collection of old garden ornaments, some dating back to the time of the first Queen Elizabeth, as well as a sunken garden, a wildflower garden, an herb garden, and camellias and azaleas in season. Open from 9:00 A.M. to 8:00 P.M. daily. Closed Saturday and Sunday in December and January. Modest admission charged.

Complete your history lesson by visiting the ◆*Elizabeth II* **State Historic Site,** across the bridge and opposite the Manteo waterfront. The museum (919–473–1144) contains exhibits depicting life in the sixteenth century, including a reproduction of a sailing vessel similar to what would have been used to bring the first colonists to Roanoke in 1585. A twenty-minute multimedia program gives you the feel of those early voyages and what it would have been like to live on the ship. In the summer, costumed actors portray early marines and colonists. After seeing the film, you may tour the ship. Open November 1 through March 31 from 10:00 A.M. to 4:00 P.M. Tuesday through Sunday (last tour begins at 3:00 P.M.). Closed Monday. Open April 1 through October 31 from 10:00 A.M. to 6:00 P.M. daily (last tour begins at 5:00 P.M.). Moderate admission is charged. Write *Elizabeth II* State Historic Site, Manteo 27954.

In downtown Manteo (named for an Indian of Roanoke who went back to England with the early sailors) on Highway 64/264, you can pick up a bit of local family history by staying at **Scarborough Inn** (919–473–3979), run by longtime residents of the

Elizabeth II

island. Six rooms in the inn and four in the annex are furnished with comfortable old furniture that has been in the family, or at least in the community, for generations. It's not fancy stuff but the kind of thing you remember from visiting old Aunt Lizzie or Great-grandma. Nearly every piece has a story that Rebecca and Fields Scarborough, who love to talk, will tell you gladly. The rooms are simple but comfortable. Two units over the barn are outfitted with king-size beds. Each room has a private bath, a small refrigerator, and a coffeemaker with coffee provided. No breakfast is served, but Rebecca leaves a couple of packs of doughnuts by the coffeemaker. Rates begin at about $50 and include use of bicycles for exploring the island.

Across the road from Scarborough Inn, the **Weeping Radish** specializes in authentic German food served by waitresses in Bavarian costume and accompanied by a variety of dark and light beers from the Weeping Radish microbrewery, all to the tune of Bavarian folk music. Open daily from 11:00 A.M. to 9:00 P.M. Tours of the brewery are available on a varying schedule (919–473–1991).

For more elegant accommodations and dining, try **Clara's Seafood Grill** on the waterfront. According to the Scarboroughs, Clara's, in the waterfront condos overlooking rows of sailboats and yachts, makes the best crab cakes in town. Advertised on the menu as "more crab than cake," these hefty crab cakes are coated with a tempuralike batter that barely contains the large lumps of crab bursting from the cake. Homemade whole-wheat rolls, an imported beer or some wine, a house salad with strawberry vinaigrette, and a rich fudge Kentucky Derby pie complete a sumptuous meal, all for about $20. The atmosphere is upscale, but casual dress is appropriate. Clara's (919–473–1727) is in the condo division at the corner of Sir Walter Raleigh and Queen Elizabeth avenues. Open daily from 11:30 A.M. to 9:30 P.M. in summer and noon to 8:30 P.M. the rest of the year. Sometimes closed for a few weeks in winter.

You might put what you don't spend at Clara's toward a special night at ◆ **Tranquil House Inn.** The inn, on the waterfront in downtown Manteo, whispers *luxury* when you enter—clearly a chocolates-on-the-pillow kind of place. The building is a reproduction of a typical nineteenth-century Outer Banks inn, with added contemporary conveniences a nineteenth-century traveler wouldn't even have dreamed about. Because of the pale cypress woodwork, glass, and stained glass throughout, the inn's inte-

39

rior seems almost as bright and sunny as the docks outside. The inn has an upscale gourmet restaurant with a fine wine list. In the guest rooms, you find not only the expected amenities such as television and telephone, but also Oriental carpets, fine furnishings, and hand-tiled bathrooms. Rates, commensurate with the luxurious atmosphere, include continental breakfast (919–473–1404 or 800–458–7069).

The other community on Roanoke Island, **Wanchese** (named for another Indian who took off for England), doesn't seem to know it is surrounded by tourists. Most of the people of Wanchese fish for a living. Driving on Highway 345 south to the village, you pass modest homes—many with a boat in the yard—battered vans, worn pickups, and lots of churches, flowers, and pets. Signs in some of the yards invite you to buy hand-carved duck decoys, driftwood, wood crafts, and nursery plants. All the people you see in the community will talk to you pleasantly and seem to enjoy your watching them work on the docks.

◈ **Fisherman's Wharf Restaurant** (919–473–5205), a large, unpretentious restaurant on the wharf, surrounded by pilings, wild stands of Queen Anne's lace, and rolls of chicken wire, specializes in broiled and fried seafood and Wanchese crab cakes at modest prices. From your table you can watch the same fishing fleets that probably caught what you're eating. Sometimes broadcasts from a religious radio station drift through a speaker at the door. No alcohol is sold or permitted on the premises. Open from noon to 9:00 P.M. Monday through Saturday, from mid-April through October or later, depending on weather.

Before you leave Roanoke Island, take time to visit this branch of the **North Carolina Aquarium,** about a mile north of Manteo, off Highway 64. Here you get a close-up view of live marine life, including sharks, eels, and sea turtles. A touch tank, as the name implies, lets you feel live crabs and starfish. Open Monday through Saturday from 9:00 A.M. to 5:00 P.M. and Sunday from 1:00 to 5:00 P.M. The aquarium maintains a full calendar of special events, from seafood-cooking workshops to field trips and cruises. For a current schedule, write the aquarium, Roanoke Island, Manteo, 27954, or call (919) 473–3493. Admission is free.

From Manteo, a short drive across the bridge on Highway 64/264 takes you to Bodie Island (which isn't really an island anymore but a location along the northern section of the Outer Banks), where it's worth stopping to see the Bodie Island Lighthouse, operating since 1872. Aside from Coquina Beach, a good beach for swimming and fishing, you won't find many attractions here. A turn to the south, however, takes you to Hatteras Island, home of the tallest lighthouse in America, the **Cape Hatteras Lighthouse.** Although the lighthouse has been in place since 1869, erosion keeps eating away at the sand on which it's built, and the National Park Service is exploring possibilities for moving it or finding some other way of protecting it. This area is undeveloped because the protected Cape Hatteras National Seashore comprises Hatteras, some of the southern end of Bodie, and Ocracoke. Here you can see natural beaches and their attendant wildlife, seashells as they wash ashore and accumulate, and vegetation dwarfed and gnarled by salt and wind but not threatened by macadam, all without water slides. For more information on the area, write the Superintendent, Cape Hatteras National Seashore, Route 1, Box 675, Manteo 27954, or call (919) 473–2111. Then at the north end of Hatteras Island, Pea Island National Wildlife Refuge, an area of nearly 6,000 acres, is a place to see more than 250 different species of birds, watch the ocean, and see old shipwrecks near shore. The refuge has observation decks about five miles south of the Oregon Inlet Bridge. For details phone the information office (919–473–1131).

It's a different story turning north from Bodie Island. You drive through the kind of beach-strip conglomeration of motels, restaurants, gas stations, fast-food chains, and beach shops that typifies most popular beach areas. As a follower of unbeaten paths, you might choose to skip it, unless you're interested in seeing the ◆ **Wright Brothers National Memorial** at Kill Devil Hills, which marks the spot where Wilbur and Orville Wright first got off the ground in powered flight on December 7, 1903. The visitors center here has full-sized copies of the brothers' glider and their first plane. The brothers' workshop and living quarters have been re-created too. Open daily from 9:00 A.M. to 7:00 P.M. Winter hours may be shorter. Modest admission charged on weekends (919–441–7430).

Kill Devil Hills is a destination resort area, probably the kind of thing you're trying to avoid. But if it seems appropriate to spend the night, try **Ye Olde Cherokee Inn Bed and Breakfast.** This big, square, blue-green beach house was run by Bob and Phyllis Combs, self-described as "a couple of Yankees from Ohio who came south to get warm." Now it is run by the Combses'

41

Cape Hatteras Lighthouse

son, also Bob, and his wife Kaye, who say the same description pretty much fits them. The Combses bought the Cherokee, which was originally a hunting and fishing lodge, from a sea captain. The six guest rooms are done in cypress, with white ruffled curtains and ceiling fans. It might surprise the sea captain that the rooms have private baths and color television. The inn is open from April through October. Rates include a continental breakfast (919–441–6127).

Once you get this far north on the Outer Banks, it makes more sense to keep driving north on Highway 158 across the bridge onto the mainland than it does to backtrack. Following Highway 158, you can pick up Highway 17 South at **Elizabeth City.** Elizabeth City merits at least a brief stop, if only because it is at the site of a canal dug in 1790 with the unlikely name of Dismal Swamp Canal. A Coast Guard installation nearby and the local shipyard make this clearly a working, rather than a vacationing, area. The town, however, has a number of interesting historical buildings that are easy to check by taking a walking tour. For a map write the Chamber of Commerce, 502 East Ehringhaus Street, P.O. Box 426, Elizabeth City 27907, or call (919) 335–4365.

The **Museum of the Albemarle** (919–335–1453), about 3 miles south of town on Highway 17, provides information on the area, known as the Historic Albemarle Area, along with displays of artifacts and exhibits related to local history. (Colonists first revolted openly against the English monarchy here.) Open Tuesday through Saturday from 9:00 A.M. to 5:00 P.M. and Sunday from 2:00 to 5:00 P.M. Closed Monday and major holidays. Admission is free.

The next community along Highway 17, Hertford, the Perquimans County seat (population only about 2,000) is on the Perquimans River, which feeds into Albemarle Sound. It's worth a stop to visit the **Newbold–White House,** believed to be the oldest house in North Carolina, probably built sometime between the early 1660s and 1685. The house has been restored, preserving much of the original handwork of the brick chimneys and walls and some of the woodwork. Though not the original, the furnishings are authentic pieces dating from the seventeenth century. Open from March to the week before Christmas, Monday through Saturday, 10:00 A.M. to 4:30 P.M. Other times by appointment (919–426–7567). Modest admission charged.

As an alternate plan if you are pressed for time, you may

decide to skip the northern Outer Banks and go back from Roanoke Island on Highway 64, which takes you across the Alligator River and through the Alligator River Refuge (it's not clear whether the refuge protects people from alligators or the other way around) where you'll find lots of wildlife, picnic areas, and boating access. Either way, make your next stop Edenton, the first capital of colonial North Carolina. From Highway 64, take Highway 32 North. On Highway 17, keep going about 15 miles west from Hertford.

CAPITAL COUNTRY

Although **Edenton** is in no way backward, it has managed to retain the calm and slower pace that we associate with earlier times and has done an outstanding job of preserving its historical sites and promulgating the facts.

Blackbeard lived here, even though he hung out in Bath and maybe left his treasure there. This would have been good pirate country. It was a busy port town in the eighteenth and early nineteenth centuries. During the Revolutionary War supplies were shipped from here to Washington's army farther north.

Edenton had some of the earliest female political activists, too. In 1774, fifty-one women gathered in the courthouse square to sign a declaration vowing not to drink English tea or wear English clothing.

To steep yourself in colonial and Revolutionary War history, you have a choice of a guided or a self-guided walking tour. Pick up a walking-tour map for a quarter, or join a guided tour for a modest fee at the **Barker House Visitors Center** (919–482–2637). A free audiovisual presentation gives you some orientation in the area's history. The Barker House (ca. 1782) was the home of Thomas Barker, a colonial agent in England, and his wife, Penelope, one of those ladies who boycotted English tea and clothing. Open Monday through Saturday from 10:00 A.M. to 4:30 P.M. and Sunday from 2:00 to 5:00 P.M. Closed Thanksgiving, Easter, December 24–26, and New Year's Day.

Call the visitors center also to arrange a guided walking tour of Historic Edenton. It takes a couple of hours. The tour includes four interesting buildings: Chowan County Courthouse, one of the oldest in the country, built in 1767; the Cupola House, noted for its elaborate Georgian woodwork inside; the James Iredell

House State Historic Site, built in 1773, home of the first attorney general of North Carolina; and St. Paul's Episcopal Church, built in 1736. You may also purchase tickets to go into individual buildings apart from the tours. Rates for the tours and buildings are modest.

Because it's so pleasant, full of flowers, friendly people, and lovely waterfront vistas, spending the night in Edenton rests and relaxes you.

◆ **The Lords Proprietors' Inn,** located at 300 North Broad Street (919–482–3641), has earned a reputation as one of the most elegant and gracious inns in the state. The inn comprises three separate restored homes in the historic district, grouped around lawn and gardens and the Whedbee House, on a brick patio, where continental breakfast is served. Each of the twenty rooms has private bath, cable television, videocassette player, and telephone. Arch and Jane Edwards, the proprietors, invite guests to use their swimming pool and to visit their private home, an authentically restored house of the 1800s. Also, they sponsor some weekend packages that include a tour of several private historic homes and a candlelight dinner.

All the guest rooms are light and airy. The common rooms have lots of open space, beautifully refinished old floors, and many whimsical decorating touches. You have the sense here of being in a professionally run inn of quality.

A few steps away, at 304 North Broad Street, Shack and Ruth Shackelford offer an entirely different lodging alternative. **Governor Eden Inn** (919–482–2072), four rooms with private bath and television in the old neoclassical family home, gives you the feeling of stopping in to spend the night with a friendly relative. Ruth and Shack are local folks who enjoy guests, like to serve tea on the balcony or downstairs verandah, and expect to sit in the parlor to chat with you. Rates include a full breakfast. Shack enjoys a joke, or as Ruth puts it, "He's always cuttin' the fool," and Ruth is a homey soul whose conversations often begin, "Honey, let me tell you . . ."

As for places to eat when you're in town, you're in for a true off-the-beaten-path experience at **Bob and Sharon's Bar-B-Que Barn** on Highway 32 on the south side of town. For the most fun, sit at one of the five tables in the front rather than in the larger dining room in back. Up front, you can enjoy the company and comments of the local workers, such as the men

45

from nearby Edenton Utilities, as they have lunch and swap wisecracks.

"Boy, did it rain or did it rain?"

"It was so bad I had to get up in the trees and swing to the truck."

The restaurant serves burgers and a variety of home-cooked platters, but the barbecue deserves first place on your list of choices. Open from 11:00 A.M. to 8:30 P.M. every day but Sunday.

A popular restaurant in Edenton is **Broad Street Restaurant & Pub**, 705 North Broad Street. This is a rustic place with knotty pine walls, serving good Italian food. Everything from the soup and entrees to the desserts are freshly prepared on the premises. Adult portions are generous; there's also a children's menu. This is a nice place to enjoy a glass of wine or a cocktail before your meal, too. The restaurant is open Monday through Friday from 11:30 A.M. to 10:00 P.M., Saturday from 5:00 to 10:00 P.M. Closed Sundays and holidays. Phone (919) 482–3902.

When you study North Carolina history, much of it seems to be about war campaigns, documents, and declarations. Two tour plantations in the area give you a more personal look at history on the day-to-day level.

◆ **Hope Plantation,** about 20 miles west, in Windsor on State Highway 308, 4 miles west of the highway bypass, re-creates rural domestic life in northeastern North Carolina during the colonial and Federal periods. The plantation belonged to Governor David Stone, who also served in the state House of Commons and later as a U. S. senator. Stone owned more than 5,000 acres, planted mostly in wheat and corn. The plantation had all the mills, shops, and work areas necessary to be self-sufficient.

The two homes on the plantation, one dating from 1763, the other from about 1803, are examples of architecture that combines medieval English, Georgian, and neoclassical traits, reflecting the changing needs and knowledge of North Carolina colonists. Touring them, you see examples of how they might have been furnished, based on research about the plantation. The project continues to develop, so that eventually you'll be able to study a reconstruction of the kitchen on its original foundation, inspect relocated and restored outbuildings, and examine historically authentic vegetable and flower gardens. Moderate admission charged. Open March through December 23, Monday

46

through Saturday from 10:00 A.M. to 4:00 P.M. and Sunday from 2:00 to 5:00 P.M. Closed Thanksgiving Day. For full information, write P.O. Box 610, Windsor 27983, or call (919) 794–3140.

The second plantation deserves much wider attention. ◆ **Somerset Place,** a nineteenth-century coastal plantation near Creswell, belonged to Josiah Collins, a successful merchant who came to Edenton from England in 1774. He and other investors formed the Lake Company, which acquired more than 100,000 acres of land next to Lake Phelps. They dug (or, more accurately, had slaves dig) a 6-mile-long canal through an area known as the Great Alligator Dismal, to join the lake to the Scuppernong River and drain the swamps. When things were going well, gristmills and sawmills produced rice and lumber to ship down the canal in flatboats. But the flooding it takes to grow rice bred mosquitoes that made the slaves sick, so eventually the plantation grew corn and wheat instead.

Collins bought out his partners in 1816 and at his death passed the property on to his son. Later, Josiah Collins III took over. It seems Josiah Three, who went to Yale and graduated from law school in Connecticut, had a head for business. He turned Somerset Place into one of the state's largest plantations, working more than 300 slaves by 1860. Most North Carolinians didn't own slaves; Collins was one of only four planters in the state with more than 300.

The great fascination in visiting Somerset Place lies in the uncommonly detailed records the Collins family kept, especially about the black people on the plantation. The records detailed not only births, deaths, and marriages, but also jobs and skills. Thus today we know that the cook was Grace and that one slave, Luke Davis, had only one job, cleaning carpets. We know that two sons of Collins III were playing with two slave boys one winter when all four boys drowned in the canal.

Additional information comes from the accounts of Dr. John Kooner, a physician who used to stay at the plantation for several weeks at a time treating the slaves and the Collins family. He described an elaborate African dance that slaves Collins had imported directly from Africa apparently taught to the rest of the slave community. They performed it every year at Christmas, beginning at the great house, snaking to the overseer's house, and ending up at the slave quarters. Everyone on the plantation participated, either as a slave dancer or a spectator.

47

Archaeological exploration has turned up the remains of slave houses, a hospital and chapel, and the plantation's formal garden as well as the original brick boundary walls.

This kind of priceless information continues to come to light at Somerset Place, where personable and knowledgeable guides work hard to pass it on. You won't experience a routinized, canned tour here.

A dramatic sidebar to this story is that Dorothy Spruill Redford, a descendant of the Somerset slave families, published a book (Doubleday, 1988) entitled *Somerset Homecoming: Recovering a Lost Heritage.* In it she details the research it took to identify and find descendants of the Somerset families, describes contacting them, and tells about the huge, emotional reunion, or more accurately, first union, they held on the plantation. Redford includes much plantation history in her book as well.

Ultimately, the Civil War did in the plantation. The Collins family died elsewhere, and today the site is run by the state.

Somerset (919–797–4560) is open April 1 through October 31, Monday through Saturday from 9:00 A.M. to 5:00 P.M., Sunday from 1:00 to 5:00 P.M.; November 1 through March 31, Tuesday through Saturday from 10:00 A.M. to 4:00 P.M., Sunday from 1:00 to 4:00 P.M. Closed Monday. These hours may vary; for details contact the site manager (P.O. Box 215, Creswell, 27928). Admission is free. At Creswell, the turn for the plantation is marked with a sign.

THE UPPER PIEDMONT

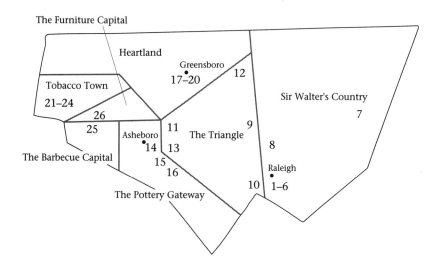

1. Historic Oakwood
2. The Oakwood Inn
3. North Carolina Museum of History
4. North Carolina Museum of Natural Sciences
5. North Carolina Museum of Art
6. Jean-Claude's Cafe
7. La Grange Plantation Inn
8. Cedar Creek Gallery
9. Duke Homestead State Historic Site and Tobacco Museum
10. B. Everett Jordan Lake
11. Womancraft
12. Hillsborough
13. Fearrington Inn
14. North Carolina Zoological Park
15. Richard Petty Museum
16. Seagrove
17. North Carolina A & T State University
18. Charlotte Hawkins Brown Memorial
19. Greensboro Historical Museum
20. Natural Science Center
21. R. J. Reynolds Tobacco U.S.A.
22. Old Salem
23. Museum of Early Southern Decorative Arts
24. Brookstown Inn
25. Lexington
26. The High Point Historical Museum

THE UPPER PIEDMONT

SIR WALTER'S COUNTRY

You should probably get here soon if you want to enjoy the Raleigh area. Although the population hovers around several thousand more or less than 200,000, depending on your source, the entire area is developing or at least spreading out rapidly, especially in the direction of Durham. Driving along rural roads, you often come upon heavy equipment and newly cleared land. Tomorrow that land will be home to a new development. But the area is rich in history, culture, and amenities that it would be a shame to skip.

Raleigh, the state capital, named for Sir Walter Raleigh, offers a variety of historical sites, museums, and fine old architecture in addition to the government buildings downtown.

Plan on stopping at ◆ **Historic Oakwood,** at North Person Street between Jones and Boundary, if you're interested in Victorian homes. This historic district of more than 400 homes, many restored, is considered one of the best examples of an unspoiled Victorian neighborhood in the country. Pick up a free walking-tour map that includes some history and descriptions of some of the buildings at the Capital Area Visitors Center, 301 North Blount Street. The center (919–733–3456) is open Monday through Friday from 8:00 A.M. to 5:00 P.M.; Saturday from 9:00 A.M. to 5:00 P.M.; and Sunday from 1:00 to 5:00 P.M. Closed Thanksgiving, December 24 and 25, and New Year's Day.

◆ **The Oakwood Inn,** 411 North Bloodworth Street, offers you an opportunity to spend the night in an 1871 Victorian home in the heart of the historic district. The proprietors, Jim and Vara Cox, know a lot about the area and keep maps with lots of information about the old houses on hand to guide you through the historic neighborhood. The inn, which has six guest rooms, is attracting increasing numbers of business travelers during the week and because of that has put telephones in every room and makes cable television available in your room if you request it. Oakwood breakfasts fall in the gourmet category: croissant French toast, pumpkin pancakes, orange waffles, and so on. Breakfast is included in the rates, beginning at about $75 for a double room.

As for the museums, two deserve your attention. The ◆ **North**

50

Carolina Museum of History concentrates on exhibits, artifacts, and dioramas related to state history, transportation, and, of course, the Revolutionary War and the Civil War. It also has good exhibits about women in North Carolina. Guided tours are available Monday through Friday, but you need a reservation. Located at 109 East Jones Street, the museum (919–715–0200) is open Tuesday through Saturday from 9:00 A.M. to 5:00 P.M. and Sunday from 1:00 to 6:00 P.M. Closed major holidays. Admission is free.

The ❖ **North Carolina Museum of Natural Sciences** is between Jones Street and Edenton at 102 North Salisbury Street (919–733–7450). Here you divide your attention between stuffed and skeletal remains of what once was and living specimens of what still is from across the state. In the whale hall, a 50-foot whale skeleton hung from the ceiling dominates the exhibits. The prize for live interest probably goes to a python. For twenty-five years, the python of note was 17-foot-long George, but he died with cancer when he was twenty-eight years old. Hapi, a mere baby at about six years and 15 feet, succeeds George. Hapi's acquisition interested North Carolinians enough to be written up in *Carolina Country* magazine. It seems she used to belong to Nannse and Richard I. Babcock, Jr., of Greenville and spent a lot of her time riding coiled up in the back window of the car, but as she grew she got too heavy to handle. The museum is pleased to have Hapi. Richard feels a little sad. "I'm going to miss him. He's been my buddy for a long time," Richard told the magazine, which is a little confusing, given that "he" is definitely a she. But maybe the Babcocks felt shy about looking. Museum hours are the same as those at the museum of history. Admission is free.

Also, allow time for the ❖ **North Carolina Museum of Art** at 2110 Blue Ridge Avenue (take the Wade Avenue exit off Interstate 40). The building, designed by the architect Edward Durrell Stone, who designed the John F. Kennedy Center in Washington, D.C. and the original Museum of Modern Art in New York, is important; so are the eight major collections. Arranged in chronological order, they cover 5,000 years of art, displaying work by artists from Botticelli to Monet to Andrew Wyeth. You'll also find exhibits of Jewish ceremonial art along with Greek and Roman sculpture. Tours are available at 1:30 P.M. A cafe and gift shop operate during museum hours. The museum (919–833–1935) is open Tuesday through Saturday from 9:00 A.M. to 5:00 P.M.

51

(until 9:00 P.M. Friday) and Sunday from 11:00 A.M. to 6:00 P.M. Closed Monday. Admission is free.

Attending to your dinner, a restaurant in the area really appeals to the kinds of people who read a book like this. ◆ **Jean-Claude's Cafe** serves country French food in a small, unassuming dining room, mostly to local folks who believe they're keeping the place a secret. The restaurant is in North Ridge Shopping Center, unlikely as that sounds for such a find. (Take the Old Wake Forest Road exit from the beltline and go north 3 miles on what becomes Falls of Neuse Avenue.) The menu includes a country pâté that could be a meal in itself; soup du jour specialties, such as cream of pumpkin; and entrees such as French sauerkraut with pork and mixed sausages to make your mouth water and bust your belt, at surprisingly moderate prices. The unquestioned favorite, however, is the salmon in puff pastry. You can order nice wines and imported beers here, too. Open Monday through Saturday from 11:00 A.M. to 2:00 P.M. and 5:30 to 9:00 P.M. Closed Sunday and holidays (919–872–6224).

People who enjoy Jean-Claude's also like the **Irregardless Cafe,** at 901 West Morgan Street. When they describe it, people tend to call it the "vegetarian restaurant," but it does serve chicken and fish as well as the vegetarian entrees. Don't be fooled by the sprouts in the salads. These aren't old hippies or young health-food nuts; they're folks who've figured out how to get the best flavor out of fresh ingredients with the least amount of doctoring. To dispel the notion that you're doing something that's good for you, you can order anything you like from the full bar. The homemade desserts will keep you on the sinful side, too. Open for lunch Monday through Friday from 11:30 A.M. to 2:15 P.M.; dinner Monday through Thursday from 5:00 to 9:30 P.M., Friday and Saturday to 10:00 P.M. Call (919) 833–9920.

If you like gardens and plants and farmers, you'll want to add two more stops to your itinerary—the **Raleigh Farmers Market** and the **North Carolina State University Arboretum.** The Farmers Market, 1301 Hodges Street in the warehouse section of town, draws crowds of locals with local fresh produce sold by truck farmers in the area. Even if you're traveling and don't want to haul a lot of carrots across the state, it's fun to wander around watching the people and sampling the wares. Depending on your taste in fresh fruits and vegetables, it might be a little more fun to visit here during spring strawberry season or summer peach time than, say, for fall turnips or winter squash, but the market is open year-round from 5:00 A.M. to 6:00 P.M., every day but Sunday. The arboretum (919–737–3132), on Beryl Street (take the Hillsborough Street exit off the beltline), grows thousands of plants from around the world. In addition to special interest areas, such as the silver and white garden and a Japanese garden, a long perennial garden shows what it's possible to grow outside in North Carolina every month. Open daily from 8:00 A.M. to dusk. Admission free.

For a nice break from the city, head north, either on Highway 1 or on Highway 401 and Highway 39, to Henderson, not far from the Virginia border, to spend the night at ◆**La Grange Plantation Inn** (919–438–2421). Dick and Jean Cornell are the proprietors and innkeepers and are outstandingly hospitable people. In 1985 the Cornells bought the historical house, built in 1770, restored it, added a new building for kitchen and dining room, put in a swimming pool and an estatelike lawn, designed gardens, and cleaned up a picturesque old family cemetery on the property. Then they grabbed a couple quick breaths and launched into the bed-and-breakfast business. The inn has five guest rooms, all with private bath, and is furnished English country style (Jean is English), with American and English antiques and reproductions comfortably arranged throughout. The parlor has a fireplace but no television; bedrooms have comfortable chairs with reading lamps; books fill shelves everywhere. The rural setting, lawn, fields, and woods that end at the edge of Lake Kerr slow you down and relax you almost instantly. One frequent guest says, "It's like an oasis. It feels like coming home." You can hike, watch birds, fish, or snooze. If your energy zooms, the Cornells can arrange for you to golf or play tennis at their country club nearby.

If you like good food, maybe you should have going-home clothes a size bigger. Jean's breakfasts, included in the rates, are creative and delicious and include several different breads and muffins. Sometimes she makes lemon curd, a British treat, to go with them. Guests known for their austerity have been caught having thirds.

While you're in the area, treat yourself to the ◆**Cedar Creek Gallery,** 1150 Fleming Road, a workplace and sales outlet for top-quality craftspeople. Their brochure says, "Expect to be overwhelmed," and that's not hype. The gallery displays are spread

53

through many rooms. Much of the work is pottery, but you'll also find fine glass, handmade stereopticons, stringed instruments, jewelry, and toys that are too splendid to put into the hands of kids. The quality is so outstanding that people tend to walk along talking in hushed tones, though that's not at all the demeanor of the artisans themselves. In the rear of the gallery, the **Museum of American Pottery** displays the entire range of local pottery, from the old folk pottery of places such as Cole and Jugtown to the works of contemporary studio potters. The exhibits include information about basic potting procedures and such things as salt glazes, too. From Henderson, go south on Interstate 85, take the second Butner exit (186), turn left on Highway 15 North, turn right at the first crossroads, and left on Fleming Road to the gallery. Open daily from 10:00 A.M. to 6:00 P.M. (919–528–1041).

As a final indulgence in this area, stop at **Bob's Bar-B-Que,** on Highway 56 between Creedmore and Interstate 85. Not only can you get good North Carolina barbecue here, but you can also dig into a serving of bunter stew, made with beef, pork, limas, and potatoes. Might as well just leave on those going-home clothes. The traditional beverage is iced tea, sweet or unsweetened, served in plastic cups with the name of the restaurant on the side. Open Monday through Saturday from 10:00 A.M. to 8:15 P.M. (919–528–2081).

THE TRIANGLE

In a sense, Durham is closer to Raleigh than it used to be. With both communities expanding laterally, it's not hard as you drive between the two places to imagine that they'll soon run together. Durham is a tobacco town; the major university, Duke University, was endowed by and named for the Duke family, which made Durham a tobacco center.

Although tobacco is not as important in the area as it once was, criticizing smokers is not a good way to make friends here. The Duke family pioneered in marketing cigarettes in America. You can understand something of the mystique and importance of tobacco by visiting the ◆ **Duke Homestead State Historic Site and Tobacco Museum,** established on the Duke family farm. Take the Guess Road exit off Interstate 85 to 2828 Duke Homestead Road. Depending on when you're here, you'll see tobacco being planted, cultivated, harvested, or prepared for market and have the opportunity to participate in part of the processing.

On the property, the old family house, two tobacco factories, a curing barn, and a packhouse show you how it used to be. In the visitors center, tobacco-related exhibits include advertising, signs, machinery, and an old cigar store Indian. A twenty-minute film, CAROLINA BRIGHT (the local name for brightleaf tobacco) describes the history and importance of tobacco in the state in a more positive light than most of what you see and hear today. Admission is free. Open April through October, Monday through Saturday from 9:00 A.M. to 5:00 P.M. Sunday from 1:00 to 5:00 P.M. and November through March, Tuesday through Saturday from 9:00 A.M. to 5:00 P.M. and Sunday from 1:00 to 5:00 P.M. Closed Monday, Christmas Day, and Thanksgiving. Hours change, so it's a good idea to call ahead (919–477–5498).

Duke money also made possible a dominant institution in this area, **Duke University.** In 1924 a $6 million gift from the family made it possible to expand what was then Trinity College. A large endowment and subsequent grants followed. The result is Duke University's two large campuses spread west and east of Durham, with great stone buildings and acres of grass and woods seeming to be enough for a huge student population. In fact, everything is large except the student body. Enrollment is in the neighborhood of 10,000 students, most of whom have to walk a lot to cover the large distances. The campuses are called, appropriately enough, East Campus and West Campus. You get to East Campus by following the signs from U.S. 15/501 bypass to State Road 751 onto Duke University Road. The Georgian buildings of the original college are here.

To get to West Campus take the Hillsborough Road exit from Interstate 85 and go east on Main Street. On the West Campus the massive Gothic **Duke University Chapel** dominates (919–684–2572). James Duke, founder of the university, planned it that way. In March 1925, when he was walking the woods that have become West Campus, he designated the highest ground as the chapel site, saying that he wanted the central building of the campus to be "a great towering church" so dominating it would have a spiritual influence on the young students who studied there. This edifice is worth a visit.

Horace Trumbauer, of Philadelphia, who designed Duke's mansion on Fifth Avenue in New York, was the architect. Chief designer was Julian Able, the first black architect graduated from the department of architecture at the University of Pennsylvania.

Duke chose to have the church built of gray stone from a quarry in nearby Hillsborough. The result is a Gothic church patterned after the original Canterbury Cathedral. A 210-foot tower soars skyward, housing a fifty-bell carillon. A 5,000-pipe organ was built into the rear of the nave several decades after the chapel's construction.

The organ, designed by Dirk Andries Flentrop of Azzndam, Holland, is an eighteenth-century organ of classical design, constructed of solid wood and using no electricity except to power the blower. It was built in Holland, where it was played to assure its quality. It was then totally dismantled, with each pipe wrapped separately, and shipped to Duke University. After the organ's first official use at Christmas, 1976, one critic wrote that the organ "breathes music." In daylight the red, green, and gold trim on its mahogany seem to combine with the glow of its 5,000 long slender pipes.

Sunlight streams through seventy-seven stained-glass windows. These and the ornamental lead and gold symbols in the doors of the building were designed and created by G. Owen and Bonawit, Inc. of New York.

Instead of kings and saints at the portals, the chapel memorializes Protestant heroes such as Luther, John Wesley, Thomas Jefferson, and Robert E. Lee.

James Duke, his brother Benjamin, and their father Washington are entombed in a small memorial chapel. Statues, showing all three men lying comfortably pillowed and gracefully draped, are carved in marble atop their tombs beneath the windows. Charles Keck of New York was the sculptor.

The elaborate ironwork of the gates to the memorial chapel was done by William H. Hackson Company of New York.

Fine woodwork throughout the building was done by Irving and Casson, A. H. Davenport Inc., Boston; the stone carving was by John Donnelly, Inc. of New York.

It may seem strange that so much work in this southern chapel was done by New York and Boston craftsmen until you realize that James Duke was living in New York when the project was in process.

Duke University Chapel

The chapel is open daily from 8:00 A.M. to 10:00 P.M. during the school year. Hours are shorter in summer. Interdenominational worship services are at 11:00 A.M. on Sundays.

The **Sarah Duke Memorial Gardens** (919–684–3698) have lots of open grass for kids to romp on and paths through wooded areas, as well as all kinds of seasonal flowers, a gazebo, and a lily pond. The gardens are open every day from 8:00 A.M. to sundown.

While you're in the Triangle, take a picnic to the ◆ **B. Everett Jordan Lake,** a 47,000-acre lake created by the United States Army Corps of Engineers for flood control. All water recreation is available at some part of the lake—boating, swimming, fishing, as well as hiking and camping. As you drive around in the area, you'll probably notice several different roads, all marked with signs, leading into access areas. One is Highway 64 at Highway 51, which leads to several recreation areas. Another is off Highway 64 going north on Highway 15/501, a point southwest of Durham, which takes you from Pittsboro, through Bynum and into Chapel Hill, home of the University of North Carolina at Chapel Hill. Chapel Hill and Durham are so close together that residents frequently live in one community and work in the other. The area south of Chapel Hill is still fairly rural and is a popular living area for university people with an itch to rusticate.

Chapel Hill, almost the geographical center of North Carolina, is recognizably a college town, the kind in which the campus and the town meet at a wall running along the campus green, where students sit on the wall to see and be seen, and where the businesses across the street are mostly campus oriented. Visitors actually tour the campus, less because of its history than because it is so Norman Rockwellish, sort of an artist's conceptualization of a campus, with trees and grass and historic buildings—even some ivy here and there.

In the college atmosphere, ◆ **Womancraft,** a retail gallery of area artisans, seems to be just what you'd expect. Forty or so craftswomen sell their work in the cooperative. The offerings range from Appalachian mountain crafts such as basketry to sophisticated stained glass and stitchery. You'll find handmade quilts, weavings, jewelry, pottery, artwork, and sculpture. The children's toys and clothes are especially popular with shoppers. The shop doesn't have the hit-or-miss feeling that tends to pervade some cooperatives, probably because it is so well established. Womancraft is entering its third decade in business.

The crafters take turns working in the shop; they hire no outside help. This means that whenever you shop, you have the opportunity to talk with some of the people who have made the things you're inspecting. Items are arranged in appealing displays throughout the space rather than each member's work being confined to a particular booth. The shop is a pleasure to visit anytime, but it is especially rewarding around holidays. They take pains to offer seasonally appropriate items for Christmas and other special times. The shop (919–929–8362) is at 1800 East Franklin Street in the East Gate Shopping Center. That's on Highway 15/501 South, east of Highway 86 heading toward Carrboro. Open Monday through Friday from 10:00 A.M. to 8:00 P.M., Saturday from 10:00 A.M. to 6:00 P.M., Sunday from 1:00 to 6:00 P.M.

Make a quick 12-mile side trip north on Highway 86 to ◆ **Hillsborough,** where a lot of history is condensed in a small area. Hillsborough was a capital of colonial and revolutionary North Carolina and a center of politics. During the Revolution, troops of Cornwallis grouped for deployment here. The state convention to ratify the federal Constitution met here in 1788; in 1865 the Confederate general who signed the surrender of the Civil War headquartered here. Colonial, antebellum, and Victorian architecture mingle comfortably along the streets. The Hillsborough Historical Society likes to say that the town is a living, not a reconstructed, community.

At the Orange County Historical Museum or the Town Hall you can pick up an annotated map for a walking tour. For further information from the historical society, phone (919) 732–8648 mornings.

South of Chapel Hill on Highway 15/501, shortly after you pass the access roads to the lake between Bynum and Pittsboro, two more women practice their craft in a ramshackle building beside the road. Neolia and Celia Cole make pottery in the North Carolina production tradition, specializing in spongeware, a soft brownish glaze called "butterware," and a shocking red glaze. The pots at **Cole's Pottery,** 3410 Hawkins Avenue, Sanford, are not the sleek stylish pieces of studio potters, but the made-for-use mugs, bowls, pitchers, and teapots of the kind that served local people for daily use in earlier days. The sisters also make a variety of miniature tea sets and vases. They sign each piece with a comment like, "Love, Neolia Cole," and "Let me go home with you."

59

Their stock, like that of most North Carolina potters, fluctuates with demand. Sometimes they can hardly keep up, and the shelves will be sparsely filled; other times pots crowd every available inch. Nobody gets upset if you stop in, look around, and leave without having bought anything. Open Monday through Friday from 8:00 A.M. to 5:30 P.M. and Saturday from 8:30 A.M. to 3:30 P.M. (919–776–9558). New potteries spring up regularly in this area and their numbers grow steadily, so when you drive through, you will certainly see signs for some items not mentioned here that will be worth a look.

In Pittsboro you need to see ◆ **Fearrington Inn** even if you can't afford to stay there. And many of us cannot! The inn is part of Fearrington Village, a remarkably tasteful planned community settled into the rural countryside, side by side with pastures and productive fields. The creators, J. B. and Jenny Fitch, mean to preserve the old Fearrington farm and its buildings, adding a new country village to the acreage. One of the first things you notice is funny-looking cows in the fields. They're belted Galloway cows from Scotland. They look as though their middles had been wrapped in Ace bandages about 2 feet wide. They're a passion of J. B. Here and there around the place you'll see little notes and signs explaining that although Galloways usually are raised for beef, these animals are Fearrington pets!

When you stay at the inn or eat at Fearrington House, a few steps away, you become part of the village. The restaurant is in the old homestead. The inn is newly built to match the homestead and decorated in English country style, with chintz and live plants and English pine antiques. Wide windows let in sunlight everywhere. The wood for the beautiful pale floors was imported from England.

If you like the inn's accessories, you'll like the gift shop, the Southern Country Garden Shop. The complex also includes Pringle Pottery, a fine studio potter, and a bookstore about which sales representatives rave. In the general store, you can pick up a gourmet lunch or supper of pasta or unusual sandwiches in the Market Cafe. For a full dinner, the award-winning Fearrington House specializes in traditional Southern foods prepared in unusual new ways: smoked quail with veal forcemeat; boneless loin of lamb with a bourbon, molasses, and butter sauce; fried sweet potatoes. Beer and wine are available. The restaurant is open Tuesday through Saturday from 6:30 A.M. to 9:00 P.M. and

Sunday from 11:00 A.M. to 2:00 P.M. The phone number for both the restaurant and inn is (919) 542–2121.

From Pittsboro it's an easy drive of no more than 40 miles west on Highway 64, mostly through rural countryside, to Asheboro. Going in every direction from Asheboro, you have wonderful possibilities.

THE POTTERY GATEWAY

Although the area bustles with activity, don't look for anything special in the way of food or lodging. Steakhouses and a few motels are about all you'll find, but these are pleasant and entirely acceptable when you just need a meal and a night's sleep, not an experience.

For an *experience,* go to the south side of Asheboro on Highway 220, where signs and arrows direct you to the ◆North Carolina Zoological Park. The zoo (910–879–7000 or 800–488–0444) is big, on more than 1,000 acres, though not all are being used yet. It's famous, and it's certainly not far off the beaten path. Go anyway. It got to be big and famous because they're doing such a good job with the concept of keeping the animals in natural environments without bars. Sometimes a natural gulf separates the people from the animals, sometimes a clear barrier. For instance, the aviary, under a glass dome, houses hundreds of exotic birds in with thousands of tropical plants. In other sections you can watch elephants, herds of antelope, and even crocodiles, all apparently blissfully unaware of an audience or confinement. Seeing everything involves walking a couple of miles or more, but for a modest fee you can ride in a tram that follows the same route as the footpaths. There is a modest admission fee. Open Monday through Friday from 9:00 A.M. to 5:00 P.M., and Saturday and Sunday from 10:00 A.M. to 6:00 P.M.

From the natural to something near the ultimate in machinery, the ◆Richard Petty Museum displays race cars, trophies, and films of famous races on the grounds of Petty's garages. Most of the awards belong to Richard, but some belong to Lee Petty, his father. Sometimes the garages are open for tours. Showcases commemorate Petty's 200th win and his 1,000th start. If you know about NASCAR racing fans, are aware of the intense partying that goes along with any race day for some of them, and have seen the huge banners advertising Goody's Headache Powders that go up at convenience stores on big race weekends, you may find humor in the Goody's Mini-Theater and Photos. Among the displays are a Chrysler Hemi engine and several race cars, all number 43. (Every car Richard Petty drives is number 43.)

Racing is so important in North Carolina that the results of all races in which local drivers participate are broadcast on local television sports news. Petty is a much-loved North Carolina hero. He has received honorary degrees from both North Carolina colleges. It would be a mistake, however, to suppose this is a uniquely North Carolina phenomenon. Among Petty's artifacts are letters of congratulations from Presidents Ford, Reagan, and Bush.

Petty's racing days have ended, but his reputation as the king of racing remains intact. Even if you neither know that Petty is the king of racing nor care a fig for the sport, you might find spending some time among people who do a fascinating cultural experience. Signs off Highway 220 near the zoo signs south of Asheboro at the Level Cross exit direct you to the museum. Modest admission fee; children under twelve free. Open Monday through Saturday from 9:00 A.M. to 5:00 P.M. (910–495–1143).

You could spend all day at the zoo; the Richard Petty Museum needs only an hour or so; the next attraction, ◆ **Seagrove,** and the potteries could take a week.

The Seagrove area is rural. You need to plan ahead for food and lodging. The nearest motels are in Asheboro, a little less than 30 miles south of Seagrove. Comfort Inn (910–626–4414) and Days Inn (910–629–2101) are at the juncture of US 64 and US 220 bypass.

Restaurants are in such short supply in pottery country that several potteries have picnic tables for shoppers who bring lunch. A good restaurant in Seagrove, on U.S. 220, is the Jugtown Cafe (910–873–8292). The food ranges from subs, croissant sandwiches and burgers to country cooking plate specials with several vegetables. The food is good and prices are moderate. The cafe is open Monday through Thursday from 5:00 A.M. to 2:00 P.M., Friday and Saturday from 5:00 A.M. to 8:00 P.M., and Sunday from 7:00 A.M. to 2:00 P.M. These hours may vary seasonally.

Before you start, accept the fact that it's physically impossible to stop at every pottery in one day. It was impossible a few years ago when they numbered in the thirties; now that there are more than fifty, your only alternatives are to choose your stops selec-

North Carolina Potters

tively or to plan several trips. New places open regularly, so don't limit your stops to those mentioned here.

Originally this part of the country attracted production potters who made the storage jugs, pitchers, crocks, and bean pots farmers used every day because both the heavy red clay for potting and the timber stands for fueling the kilns were right here. No doubt local moonshine was one of the products that got stored in the jugs. A rich culture developed around potting, complete with family traditions in design and glazing. Some, such as Ben Owens, earned reputations for being excellent turners.

As other materials came along for making utensils to cook and store food, the potters turned more to producing items for

63

tourists. But the actual potting stayed basically the same. Over three and four generations, feuds and disagreements came up, and sometimes a member of a famous potting family, such as Owens, would splinter off to start an independent pottery.

The old families continue making the same kinds of pottery today. Tourists and gift shop owners buy it up faster than the wheels at Cole and Jugtown and Owens can turn.

Newcomers fill out the scene with more artistic studio pottery, which is usually more elaborately shaped, decorated, and glazed. These pieces take longer to make.

Some of the new potters are local young people who have studied in the well-respected program at the Troy Technical College nearby. Others, transplants from elsewhere, have been attracted by the concentration of potters that draws customers and ensures support. It would be wrong to say that all new potters make studio pottery and all old-timers practice production pottery, however. You'll find a good bit of crossover. The best thing to do is simply look at the work, talk to the potters, and make your choices.

Many of the materials these days are shipped in from elsewhere rather than dug from local ground, and some kilns are fired by oil, gas, or electricity rather than wood. But the atmosphere is still that of a unique culture engrossed in a hands-on kind of work.

Some people say the old-timers don't think much of the new crowd because they're too fancy. Some people say the newcomers look down on the "production mentality" of the old families. Those attitudes may exist, but what you'll usually hear is encouragement from the long-established potters for the new ones, and deep respect and admiration from the newer people for the speed and accuracy with which a good production potter can turn. As one young man said, "I've been futzing with this lid for two hours now. Those guys would've finished a dozen pots in that time."

Wherever you stop, talk to the people. They're used to it, they like it, and it's an integral part of the experience. As you do, you can't help noticing the arthritic hands of some of the old potters. As a younger artisan explained it, "My pots will never be quite as good as theirs, because you need to keep wetting the clay with *cold* water for the very best results, and I use warm water. I've seen what twenty and thirty years of cold water and clay does to your hands. I'm afraid I'm not quite that dedicated."

The largest concentration of potteries begins on Highway 705, off Highway 220. The state road numbers are clearly marked, so it is easy to follow the map through the countryside, traveling from one pottery to another. No two are alike, nor are their wares. Part of the fun is in the discovery and surprise; you don't need full information ahead of time about each place, but following are a few guaranteed to be special. They are all marked on the free maps available at every pottery.

Phil Morgan Pottery (910–873–7304) features Phil's elegant crystalline glazes on porcelain and his wife's more traditional earthenware, much of it in pleasing muted rose and blue tones decorated with flowers. These people love to talk and can give you what seems like a complete course in the intricacies of crystalline glazing.

J. B. Cole Pottery (910–873–7171) has a huge expanse of tables and shelves in the requisite old frame building. If you can get here in early spring, March or earlier, after they've had time to stock up from the Christmas rush, the shelves and tables are laden with earthenware dinner plates, sandwich plates, bowls, pitchers, and other items in a variety of colorful glazes. A glossy deep blue and a pebbly white are probably most commonly associated with Cole's. The operation is not as big as it used to be. Some of the younger people have left to start their own potteries. This place is still interesting, though. There's a public bathroom here, which becomes more important than you'd guess driving through the countryside.

Potts Town Pottery (910–879–4295) is a new endeavor by Jeff and Linda Potts. Linda's grandmother was a Cole—the Potts say they represent the ninth generation of Coles. They use local clay and produce traditional earthenware tableware and serving pieces. Some of the glazes, especially the blue, resemble those of the Cole pottery, but you will see differences in sheen.

Ben Owens Pottery (910–464–2261) displays the work of Ben Owens III, who was recognized as a boy for having superior talent, on a par with that of his grandfather. Young Ben works as an artist, producing shapes and designs inspired by Egyptian and Japanese work. His pots are on display in museums around the country. The display rooms usually aren't heavily stocked, but you do find an interesting variety, presided over by a proud papa who can explain Ben's work in detail.

At **Westmoore Pottery** (910–464–3700), open only since 1977,

Mary and David Farrell make reproductions of the earthenware and salt-glazed stoneware typical of the eighteenth and early nineteenth centuries. They also make stunning reproductions of Moravian pottery as well as create new designs in the old traditions.

Mary can throw a pot or apply a Moravian-design slip trail without a flaw and chat with customers at the same time. The couple and the pottery have received national attention in more than one country-oriented magazine for their work and the unique new home they built behind their new pottery. Their work is especially popular with people involved in authentic historic restoration and representation.

The people at **Cady Clay Works** (910–464–5661), John Mellage and his wife, Beth Gore, produce pieces with vibrant colors and contemporary designs. They usually have some spectacular, extra-large bowls that are surprisingly lightweight for their size.

At **Walton's Pottery** (910–879–3270), Don and Susan Walton make lead-free stoneware pottery that you can safely subject to the oven, microwave, and dishwasher. The Waltons have some gorgeous glazes and unique contemporary designs. They make some small, oval dishes with straight sides that are just right for individual servings of gratineed casserole-type foods. Also, you can buy some unusual jewelry, such as earrings—hand cut, glazed, and fired—here.

DirtWorks Pottery (910–873–8979, closed Monday in January and February), is the permanent showroom of Dan Triece. Triece has won awards in the Southeast, especially for his copper luster raku. He works also in stoneware, ranging from pastels to midnight blue. The shop also carries woodcrafts, basketry, jewelry, and other North Carolina crafts as well as work by other regional potters.

Turn and Burn (910–873–7381), produces unusual hand-carved face jugs and snake jugs inspired by jugs made locally in the 1600s satirizing political problems. David Garner, who says he grew up so surrounded by the craft he can't remember the first time he saw a pot made, has been potting for twenty years, the past eight in his current location. His current favorite jug shows Ross Perot's face upside down.

Milly McCanless of **Dover Pottery** (910–464–3586) is one of the new potters, too. Initially, she got into it because she had a dollhouse and wanted to learn to throw miniature pots for her miniature dining table. In the process she discovered that she was also good with big pots. She saw that while there wasn't much market for miniatures, she could sell as much full-sized pottery as she could produce. She's especially known for pieces beautifully decorated in painted floral and bird designs. "It's functional art. I love the idea," she says. Millie's husband, Allen, has been working with crystalline and raku glazes and has some handsome pieces for sale. Sharon Williams is also a working potter at Dover. Often when you stop, you are helped by one of the McCanless children.

Jugtown (910–464–3266) operates somewhat more commercially than the other potteries, including handwoven rugs and placemats, handmade toys, and other North Carolina folk crafts in its retail stock. The Jugtown stoneware is uniform enough in appearance to look nice beside the more regular, mass-produced commercial dinnerware and seems practically indestructible. Most of the pieces reflect traditional local styles and glazes. There is a bathroom here, too. That may seem like a small thing, in the abstract, but after you've spent some time driving these country roads where you don't find pit stops every few miles, it's something to appreciate. You may also enjoy eating your picnic lunch at the tables under the trees provided for visitors.

The hours of the various potters may vary by a half-hour or so in opening and closing, but most are open from 8:30 A.M. to 4:30 P.M. Monday through Saturday. Nearly all are closed Sunday. The best time to go is Friday afternoon, when most of the kilns are opened to bring out the new pots. Saturday morning is a good time, too, but by afternoon the wares will already be thinning out. It's almost a waste of time to go around Christmas or in late summer. The shoppers then simply buy faster than the potters can pot.

Although some early glazes contained lead, today's are lead-free and safe for table use. If you have any concerns about lead, ask in the pottery.

HEARTLAND

Another possible trip from Asheboro is the short hop up Highway 220 to **Greensboro,** a pleasant city with a historic downtown and lots of surprises. There's some Revolutionary War history here, in a strange sort of way. Cornwallis won a battle against General Nathanael Greene's American troops, but in the process lost so many men that he ultimately had to surrender at York-town. The Guilford Courthouse National Military Park, 6 miles north of Greensboro on Highway 220, commemorates the loss and the win with exhibits on the battlefield and displays and films in the visitors center (910–288–1776). The center is open daily from 8:30 A.M. to 5:00 P.M. The gate to the tour road closes at 4:30 P.M. Admission is free.

Drawing on more recent events, Greensboro holds special significance for blacks. In 1960 black students from ◆**North Carolina A & T State University** (originally the Agricultural and Mechanical College for the Colored Race) began the first sit-ins at Woolworth's segregated lunch counter. A & T is Jesse Jackson's alma mater, and he still comes to town from time to time.

On the campus of North Carolina A & T State University, the Mattye Reed African Heritage Center displays African masks, paintings, black history books, and art objects. Open Monday through Friday. Call for current hours (910–334–7874). Admission is free.

Less than 10 miles east of Greensboro, the ◆**Charlotte Hawkins Brown Memorial** (910–449–4846), a still-developing state historic site, honors Dr. Brown's fifty years as head of another school for blacks, Palmer Memorial Institute. The buildings are gradually being restored, and plans are to make the memorial a center for contributions of North Carolina blacks, including a research center with collection and computer facilities devoted to North Carolina black history. Dr. Brown's house has been restored, and some of her original furniture is being reupholstered. Open Monday through Saturday from 9:00 A.M. to 5:00 P.M., Sunday from 1:00 to 5:00 P.M. April through October. Winter hours are Tuesday through Saturday from 10:00 A.M. to 4:00 P.M. and Sunday from 1:00 to 4:00 P.M. Admission is free. For further information on development of the site, write P.O. Box B, Sedalia 27342.

Local history from the time of the early Indians to date shapes the displays at the ◆**Greensboro Historical Museum,** 130 Summit Avenue, in what used to be the First Presbyterian Church. In a re-creation of nineteenth-century Greensboro, the museum shows a general store, the drugstore where William Sydney Porter (O. Henry) once worked, a post office, a law office, a firehouse, a cobbler's, and a blacksmith's.

Other exhibits include room settings from historical homes, an exhibit of household items and clothing of Dolley Madison (a

Greensboro native before she became First Lady), and a collection of antique automobiles. Open Tuesday through Saturday, 10:00 A.M. to 5:00 P.M., and Sunday from 2:00 to 5:00 P.M. (910–373–2043). Admission is free.

One stop that could be a treat for those who love dollhouses and miniatures is **Portrait House,** the photography studio of Vivian Robinson. In addition to exhibits of her photography and paintings by her husband, Stan, Vivian displays a fully land-scaped Edwardian estate that she created in the inch-to-the-foot scale. A formal wedding party fills the lawn around the gazebo and fountain. An overweight cook and a sour-faced butler that she sculpted and dressed preside over the elegant wedding buffet. Altogether, Vivian dressed twenty-two dolls in Edwardian cos-tumes. The dogwoods and redbuds are in full bloom; goldfish swim in the pond. Vivian ingeniously created realistic-looking trees and shrubs and even carved a copy of a Lutyens bench by hand. And just to show that she had the Victorians in perspec-tive, she settled Mary Poppins, umbrella, suitcase, and all, atop the chimney. Vivian says that she would sell the project, so you'd better call ahead to be sure it's still there if you'd like to see it, but you probably won't be disappointed, because she has put a super-calafragilistic price on it (910–454–5978).

If you're traveling with kids (or even if you're not, come to think of it), don't miss the ◆**Natural Science Center,** 4301 Lawndale Drive (910–288–3769), where you can easily spend a day immersing yourself in the sights and sounds of everything from dinosaurs to star systems. This is a "participation museum," where you don't have to tell the kids to look, not touch. For instance, you can put your hand into a real dinosaur footprint, pet and feed animals in the zoo, observe sunspots in the live solar observatory, and turn your imagination loose in the plane-tarium. The transparent anatomical mannequin, which you might want to save until after lunch, lets you study what goes on inside the skin of the human body. The museum is open Monday through Saturday from 9:00 A.M. to 5:00 P.M. and Sunday from 1:00 to 5:00 P.M. The zoo is open Monday through Saturday from 10:00 A.M. to 4:30 P.M. and Sunday from 12:30 to 4:00 P.M. A modest admission fee covers the museum and zoo. Planetarium shows daily at 3:00 P.M. are $1.00 extra.

Drop your weary head on a pillow at the Greenwich—a small,

older, European-style hotel downtown—or at the Greenwood Bed and Breakfast, in one of Greensboro's first suburban areas, about 10 blocks from the business district. **The Biltmore-Greensboro Hotel,** 111 West Washington Street (910–272–3474), has had what the cliché makers would call "a checkered past." It was built to be corporate headquarters for a textile company in the 1800s, then was used as a post office, and later was turned into a hospital during World War II. In the twenty years before it was rescued and renovated, it had been either a house of ill repute or a flophouse, depending on whose story you believe. A little of both may have been true. Now the lobby is a pretty little area of brass and crystal chandeliers and eighteenth-century reproductions and art. The rooms are tasteful and comfortable, with small refrigerators to cool your traveling comestibles.

The **Greenwood Bed and Breakfast,** 205 North Park Drive, Greensboro (910–274–6350 or 800–535–9363), a stick-style home built in the early 1900s, has also been renovated. Old oaks and the neighborhood park surround the home with greenery and shield the backyard swimming pool from the curious. Inside, wood carvings and art collections from around the world attract your attention. The hostess, Jo Anne Green, serves a continental breakfast with fruit and homemade breads, which is included in the rates. The inn has three guest rooms and a two-room suite, all with private baths.

TOBACCO TOWN

From Greensboro, you're looking at a drive of only about 20 miles west on Interstate 40 to Winston-Salem, the tobacco town. It would be hard to overstate the influence of the R. J. Reynolds Tobacco Company. While Richard Joshua Reynolds was directing a rapidly growing business and hiring increasing thousands of people in the tobacco factories, his wife, Katharine, set about a long series of community improvement activities for the benefit of those same families. With Reynolds money and Moravian artistic influence, the area developed into a cultural center that still ranks high in the country today.

Perhaps the most audacious Reynolds act in later years was the lock-stock-and-barrel move of Wake Forest University from Wake County to Winston-Salem in 1950. President Truman came to wield the shovel in the groundbreaking ceremony.

To learn more about the tobacco industry and the Reynolds influence in it, stop at the ❖ **R. J. Reynolds Tobacco U.S.A.** plant 3 miles north of Greensboro on Highway 52 for a guided tour of the plant that produces 450 *million* cigarettes a day, and a stop in the museum that depicts the development of the industry. Notice the heavy sweet smell of tobacco that permeates the air. Line workers who are close to the actual tobacco products will tell you that the smell gets into their clothes and remains so strong that after work at home they may shuck their work clothes at the doorway to keep the smell out of the house.

As background on the R.J.R. dynasty, you should read the recent book by Patrick Reynolds (who has come out strongly against using tobacco) and Tom Shachtman, *The Gilded Leaf: Triumph, Tragedy, and Tobacco—Three Generations of the R. J. Reynolds Family and Fortune.* Larry Hagman (who played ruthless J. R. Ewing in the "Dallas" television series) wrote that it made Dallas look "like a bowl of warm milk toast." Be careful about trying to discuss the book while you're here, though. Criticizing tobacco in a community built upon it rouses the ire of some residents. So does speaking ill of the First Tobacco Family.

About half a century ago, the town was shocked when Zachary Smith Reynolds, usually called Smith, son of R. J. and Katharine, was shot through the head during a boozy party at the family home, less than a year after his marriage to the torch singer Libby Holman. Apparently Smith Reynolds caught Libby flirting (or more) with a friend, fighting erupted, and Smith either shot himself or was killed by Libby. Newspapers suppressed much of the story at the time, and even today, polite society doesn't talk about it, though that hasn't stopped brazen authors from writing about it. An interesting source, should you decide to pursue the subject further, is the biography entitled *Libby Holman: Body and Soul,* by H. D. Perry.

After studying the impact of Reynolds and tobacco, turn your attention to the Moravians. Moravians came from Pennsylvania to settle the area in 1753. They built Salem as a totally planned, church-governed community in 1766. Winston wasn't founded until 1849. In Salem, arts and crafts flourished; in Winston, it was tobacco and textiles. By the early 1900s, the two towns had grown together and consolidated. It would be hard to say whether tobacco or the Moravians left the greater mark on the area, nor is it really pertinent; in the early days tobacco wasn't a dirty word, and nobody saw anything wrong with a strong relationship between church and chew.

If you see only one attraction here, it certainly should be ◆ **Old Salem,** a Moravian town restored so carefully that when you walk the streets and go into the buildings, you feel as though you've entered a time warp. To give you an idea of the pains staff people take with getting it right, people responsible for demonstrations of cooking and household activities take turns preparing research papers and consulting old diaries, journals, and letters to discover exactly how the households might have run. Unlike traditional historians who mainly study battles, politics, and industrial development, these re-creators also try, as well, to piece together the elements of day-to-day life. This isn't the only historic site where such activities are going on, but it's hard to imagine one where they're being treated any more earnestly or where the subject matter is any more fascinating. This attention to detail extends even to the food cooked from old Moravian recipes. The original recipe used fresh ginger root, but gingerbread recipes in later years have shifted to powdered ginger because it's easier to find and keep. The Old Salem recipe still specifies fresh, grated ginger.

Costumed guides in the old kitchen cook in the huge fireplace and iron with flatirons heated there, all the while sweating genuine sweat—a fascinating reminder in this age of air-conditioning that just getting from one day to the next took a lot of energy. Among the demonstrations offered in Old Salem are music from an organ built in 1797, potting, baking, and spinning.

Not all the buildings in the historic district are restored as tour buildings. Some are private homes. The presence of automobiles and real people living real lives doesn't seem to detract from the atmosphere; indeed it simply makes it feel more alive. Whatever tours you take, start at the visitors center (910–721–7300). Moderate to high admission fees, depending on how many features you wish to tour. Get tickets for all Old Salem tour attractions at the visitors center, open from 9:00 A.M. to 5:00 P.M. Monday through Saturday and from 12:30 to 5:00 P.M. on Sunday.

Having toured Old Salem, you'll need to eat at the **Old Salem Tavern Dining Rooms** at 736 South Main Street in the district (910–748–8585). Continuing the sense of reenactment, costumed staff serve Moravian-style cooking by candlelight. Specialties include game and gingerbread from the old recipes. For the faint of palate, standard beef and chops entrees are also available. All spirits served. The restaurant is open for lunch from 11:30 A.M. to 2:00 P.M. Sunday through Friday and from 11:30 A.M. to 2:30 P.M. Saturday; for dinner from 5:30 to 9:00 P.M. Monday through Thursday and from 5:30 to 9:30 P.M. Friday and Saturday.

Also in Old Salem, the ❖**Museum of Early Southern Decorative Arts** (910–721–7360 or 800–441–5305) gives you a close look at the results of extensive research into the regional decorative arts of the early South. The exhibits include furniture, paintings, textiles, ceramics, silver, and other metalware. You can't just wander in here. Guides take you through the building in small groups. You may buy tickets at the Old Salem Visitors Center. Museum hours are Monday through Saturday from 10:30 A.M. to 5:00 P.M. and Sunday from 1:30 to 5:00 P.M. You can spend the night in old Salem at the 1840 **Augustus T. Zevely Inn,** a privately owned bed and breakfast at 803 South Main Street. This fine old brick building is furnished with pieces of the Old Salem Collection, so that it feels much as it would have in the 1840s. Some of the twelve guest rooms have fireplaces. Some also have microwaves, refrigerators, and whirlpools which, of course, feel nothing at all like the 1840s but are kind of nice after a day of

Old Salem

walking. Rates begin at about $80 per double room. Phone (910) 748–9299 or (800) 928–9299.

An alternative end to a day in this historic manufacturing and artistic town is a night's lodging at ◆ **Brookstown Inn,** a restored 1837 textile mill (910–725–1120 or 800–845–4262). The history of the inn matches that of the city for interest. Moravians opened the Salem Cotton Manufacturing Company and later sold it, and the buildings were subsequently used as a flour mill and then as a moving-company storage house. The conversion to an inn created large guest rooms with odd nooks and crannies and high ceilings. An upstairs wall is covered with the graffiti (protected by an acrylic plastic sheet) of the young factory girls who boarded there. A boiler room with catwalk now serves as a restaurant in which one of the old boiler faces is a focal point. The decor is early American, with many handmade quilts and country accents. Rates include wine and cheese in the parlor, homemade cookies and milk, and continental breakfast in the dining room.

As you leave the area, to move swiftly back into the twentieth century you might stop at the **Sciworks,** 7½ miles north of the intersection of Interstate 40 on Highway 52 on Museum Drive off the Hanes Mill Road exit. The participatory exhibits cover natural science and physical science and technology. A three-dimensional solar system display puts you in the middle of the planets, and a model of the moon shows the landing sites of Apollo. Children especially enjoy the saltwater touch tank and the petting zoo. Modest admission fee. The museum (910–767–6730) is open Monday through Saturday from 10:00 A.M. to 5:00 P.M. and Sunday from 1:00 to 5:00 P.M. The second Friday of every month is free from 4:00 to 8:00 P.M.

THE BARBECUE CAPITAL

Also on Highway 52, about 20 miles south, the town of ◆ **Lexington** is a must-stop for barbecue freaks. More than a dozen different restaurants in this little town serve pork barbecue (if it's made with anything else it isn't really barbecue!) "Lexington style," which means a pepper-vinegar sauce. Elsewhere in the state, the sauce, which is always added later rather than simmered with the pork, contains only hot pepper and vinegar. And it never, never contains mustard. That's South Carolina barbecue. Sometimes you'll see signs in other parts of North Carolina advertising Lexington barbecue, but as anyone in town will tell you, to be authentic, it's got to be made by roasting pork shoulder over a wood fire in Lexington. And that's just the way it is.

THE FURNITURE CAPITAL

High Point is mostly about manufacturing and selling furniture. The town, already active in the lumber business, first got into furniture building in the early 1880s when a local lumber salesman noticed the big difference between the price of wood as it left the sawmill and the price it brought once it had been shipped away and turned into furniture. Sensibly, he and two local merchants risked all they had to start a furniture company close to the source of the wood. It was the right idea in the right place at the right time. Sales took off and the future was set. Today High Point has 125 furniture manufacturing companies.

Unless you are professionally involved in the furniture business, avoid High Point in April and October, when for the better part of two weeks in both months the town hosts the Southern Furniture Market, usually referred to simply as "market." Said to be the largest furniture show in the world (it fills 150 buildings and between five and six million square feet), this trade show attracts interior decorators and furniture retailers—in other words *buyers*—from all over the world. More than 1,500 furniture company exhibitors show up for each market show. Multiply that by the staff each company brings to work the booths and add all the buyers who come looking for the latest goodies, and you get an image of a town, normal population on the shy side of 70,000, so overloaded that if it were a ship it would sink. Finding a place to stay or to eat is a challenge.

A valuable museum in the area is the **Springfield Museum of Old Domestic Art,** established in 1935 in the third meetinghouse of the Springfield Meeting, 555 East Springfield Road (910–889–4911). Museums, like history books, tend to focus on extraordinary events, wars, and politics and not on the commonplaces of day-to-day life. This museum is an exception. Here you can inspect the artifacts of daily life that were used in the neighborhood for the past 200 years or more—spinning equipment, utensils, farm items, clothing, pictures from homes, toys, and a slew of fascinating odds and ends. The curator, Brenda Haworth, says, "Most of what we have has been donated by local Quakers."

75

Mrs. Haworth likes to emphasize most of the items that were so commonplace in their day, objects crudely made to fill an immediate need. If you didn't know the way in which many of them had been used, you probably could never figure out what they were for. Such artifacts simply cannot be replaced.

One example is the log lifter. It looks like a crutch for a giant. Log lifters were devices created to get logs from the ground to high points in the walls when building log cabins. One man stood at each end of the log with a lifter and heaved.

Another example is a homemade Noah's Ark, with all the animals two-by-two. This was a Sunday toy, made during the time when children in the community weren't allowed to play on Sundays with their regular toys or do much else. It was carved about 100 years ago by Yardley Warner for his twins, probably because he sympathized with the children's restlessness and wanted to make them a religious toy to keep them occupied on Sundays.

Another uncommon exhibit is the 4-foot-long tin horn the coachman blew at each stop of the stagecoach along the Old Plank Road. The number of blasts blown told people at upcoming stops, such as Nathan Hunt Tavern, what passengers would be wanting when they got there. Old Plank Road was built between Fayetteville and Winston-Salem by laying down boards next to one another to form a firm-surfaced highway. Part of the old road is now Main Street. A plank from the road and a notched mile marker are also in the display. A traveler in the dark could stop at the marker and feel the number of notches on it to know how far it was to Nathan Hunt Tavern. A model shows a stagecoach on a plank road with markers to give you an idea how it all worked.

As Brenda Haworth observes, visiting here is more like going into an attic than a museum. "There's so much stuff and you can handle it. You don't get the feeling of things resting on velvet that you can't touch," she says. The museum is open by appointment. Admission is free.

The ◆ **High Point Historical Museum**, 1805 East Lexington Avenue (910–885–6859), exhibits more traditional kinds of material related to the town's history, including military displays. There also are a display of old telephones that takes you back to before Ma Bell, a collection of furniture made in High Point, and, appropriately, woodworking tools that take you back to the first manufacturing in town. Also on the property are the restored 1786 John Haley House, a weaving house, and a blacksmith shop. Demonstrations are offered in these buildings on weekends. The museum is open Tuesday through Saturday from 10:00 A.M. to 4:30 P.M. and Sunday from 1:00 to 4:30 P.M. Other buildings are open only on weekends. Admission is free.

A pleasant place to stay while you're in High Point is **The Premier,** a six-room bed-and-breakfast inn at 1001 Johnson Street (910–889–8349). It's a completely renovated 1907 neo-Colonial home in the center of High Point's historic district. The house used to be known as Mrs. Jones's house and accommodated female schoolteachers in what were considered modest quarters then. The ladies would scarcely recognize the place today.

The decor is luxurious and eclectic, reflecting the taste of a good designer with a flash of humor. Old botanical prints and Dali prints hang side by side in rooms with classic quilts, Oriental rugs, antique wicker, and comfortable contemporary chairs. The colors lean toward pastels, grays, and white, with surprising splashes of turquoise. In one downstairs bedroom, four huge white posts that were originally part of the side porch mark the four corners of a luxuriously festooned bed. The posts are painted so that blooming vines seem to grow toward the ceiling.

Breakfast is lavish, with lots of fresh fruit, the inn's now-famous French toast (one version of which has Bailey's Irish Cream in the batter), and other out-of-the-ordinary entrees.

Partly because of the efforts of a previous innkeeper, the house is surrounded with good perennial borders, so that you enjoy peonies, foxglove, daisies, and the like, brightening the area along the privet hedge. The back doorstep of the house looks toward the historic district, which features in its old buildings a growing number of specialty shops, including a children's shop, a nature shop, a bookstore, and a gourmet shop. Whatever stores are in business when you visit here, the "boutique row" is always fun to browse through.

The inn has attracted celebrities but has done it so quietly that folks didn't know they were in town. Cher is reported to have stayed here. While it's easy to see that she would enjoy the inn, one wonders what in the world she was doing in High Point in the first place.

Within walking distance of the inn, you can dine at **Noble's,** at 114 South Main Street (910–889–3354), a restaurant described by one local resident as "nouvelle American but kind of French and almost four-star." You'll find such offerings as grilled salmon with lobster sauce, veal with chef's sauce, and game such as quail or pheasant, always prepared interestingly. The restaurant has a full liquor license and an excellent wine list. Open Monday through Wednesday, from 6:00 to 10:00 P.M. and Thursday through Saturday from 6:00 to 11:00 P.M.

A five-minute drive takes you to another popular restaurant, the **Atrium Cafe** (910–889–9934), in the furniture mall at 430 South Main Street. The prices are reasonable for outstandingly good food. The restaurant serves the specialties you'd expect—chicken, seafood, and so on—but it is famous for its duck. All spirits are available if you're thinking of making it the kind of special meal that just demands a certain drink or a glass of wine. The restaurant is fairly new and hours may change. Call ahead.

THE LOWER PIEDMONT

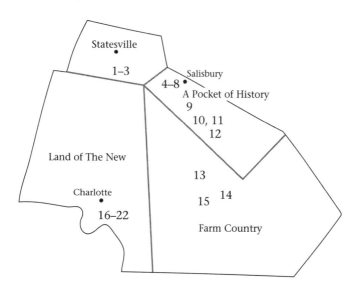

Statesville
•
1–3

Salisbury
4–8 •
A Pocket of History
9
10, 11
12

Land of The New

Charlotte
•
16–22

13

15   14

Farm Country

1. Farm House Gardens
2. Gluttons
3. Arts and Science Center
4. Historic Salisbury
5. Dr. Josephus Hall House
6. Rowan Museum
7. Waterworks Visual Arts
   Center
8. Rowan Oak House
9. Kluttz Piano Factory
10. Rockwell
11. Darrell's Bar-BQ
12. Greendale

13. Motel Restaurant
14. Cline's Country Antiques
15. Reed Gold Mine
16. The Homeplace
17. Mint Museum of Art
18. Hezekiah Alexander Homesite
19. Discovery Place
20. Pewter Rose
21. Dilworth Brewing Company
22. Schiele Museum of Natural
    History and Planetarium

THE LOWER PIEDMONT

STATESVILLE

In less than an hour, you can drive west on Interstate 40 from Winston-Salem to Statesville, where you'll find several delightful stops known mostly to local folks. ◆ **Farm House Gardens** is on the east side of town on Highway 70 (704–873–2057). If you like gardening and houseplants, you'll find that you simply must buy some plants here, even if it means driving 500 miles home with them in the back seat. Kay Kincaid, the main Farm House gardener, started the business about ten years ago with the encouragement of her husband, Randy, as the obvious expression of her lifelong passion for plants. "I always loved plants. So did my mother and before her, my grandmother. When I was little, I spent all my time around the farm at my grandmother's knees in the garden," she says. The force of that passion produced a nursery–greenhouse–gift shop combination that stuns you with the variety and quality of the offerings. This isn't the kind of place where anybody counts the number of plants for sale or measures in terms of how many greenhouses are open (that number changes with the seasons anyway).

Farm House Gardens surely isn't the largest retail plant operation in North Carolina, but it is the place you go for the special plants you haven't been able to find anywhere else. In spring, you can buy tomato plants and pepper plants, but that's rather like choosing peanut butter in a gourmet shop. The perennials fill benches and the spaces under them and are lined up along the paths of the back gardens. In the greenhouses, houseplants, including little myrtle topiaries and several different maidenhair ferns, tempt you to exceed your budget with every step you take. All the common herbs and many more that are hard to find are here, too, along with Japanese maples in great variety, enough different hostas to fill a small catalog, and rare dwarf shrubs. One gardener, nursing sore feet the day after a visit to Farm House Gardens, complained that she'd been there for four hours and hadn't seen everything.

As if the variety weren't enough, you deal with people who so obviously love and know the plants that it's more like swapping cuttings with Aunt Elizabeth than a commercial transaction. If you mistakenly zero in on a not-for-sale stock plant and are crushed that you can't have it, Kay or one of her helpers will cut off a little start for you and tuck it into the soil of another plant you've purchased, along with instructions, if you need them, on how to root the slip. If you're one who boasts that you have a black thumb and can kill anything, don't go here. They mean for your plants to thrive, and any other attitude would be an insult. Open from 9:00 A.M. to 5:00 P.M. Monday through Saturday. Closed Sunday. Write Route 7, Box 27, Statesville 28677.

A fun place for lunch or dinner has the unlikely name ◆ **Gluttons** (704–872–6951). Lots of young business people eat here. The place is trendy and a little noisy but always full of activity and fun. The copper tabletops rest on old treadle sewing machine bases. Stained glass and some wall decorations that look like they're hand drawn on rice paper, though they're not, provide you with interesting things to look at in every direction. Sometimes after dinner a roving magician stops at your table to pull off some very convincing sleight of hand.

As for the menu, lots of fresh salads and homemade dressings help ease your conscience if you go for the chef's special pork ribs or the Garden Sampler, fresh garden vegetables batter-fried and served with a dipping sauce. Other possibilities include wings fixed in several different ways, steaks, and broiled seafood and chicken. Gluttons has Killian's Irish Red beer on tap and offers good wines by the glass. To get there, take the Broad Street exit off Interstate 77 to Newton Plaza (1539 East Broad Street). Open for lunch, Monday through Friday from 11:30 A.M. to 2:30 P.M., and for dinner, Monday through Saturday from 5:00 to 10:00 P.M.

Don't leave Statesville without seeing the ◆ **Arts and Science Center,** 1335 Museum Road (704–873–4734). This is a truly local museum, and the story of its beginning and growth makes you feel good. The center is housed in a turn-of-the-century building that was the Statesville waterworks until 1940. In 1956 a group of local citizens decided that the area needed a museum and put their energy and money into making it happen. Today it operates with a $100,000-a-year budget that allows for three full-time professionals on the staff. Enthusiasm for it practically shoots out the ears of Cynthia Hanson, the director. The museum features ten temporary exhibits a year, runs thirty-five educational programs in association with the local school system each year, and displays 3,000 objects in the permanent collection. The glassware pieces number over 1,000. Cynthia says the quality of the items varies, but she feels it's important to have it all. "Somebody has to save all those Avon pieces," she says. Plans for the future include identifying all the glassware. A geologist has already put in a marathon rock-identification day to tag and group the 500 rocks in the collection.

In the small toy-and-doll collection, you'll see a Victorian doll with brown eyes—a rarity, because Queen Victoria had blue eyes, and most dolls were modeled on her.

One of the museum's founders insisted that it deal with science as well as art to attract people not interested in the arts. To help fill that need, two partly restored pioneer cabin sites have been included. Nature trails have been developed outside for short walks.

Cynthia gets most excited about the art exhibits. "We're getting really good quality exhibits because the setting is so wonderful— a pretty spot on thirty-five acres in the Piedmont by a creek." The staff has high hopes of getting an exhibit by Dr. Selma Burke, a well-known black sculptor in her late eighties, who was born nearby in Mooresville. Cynthia also plans to put together an exhibit on art in the workplace that will be created by asking industry to supply products to use in collages and other works.

But what captures the imagination of the public here is the homeless mummy. Well, it has a home now, but nobody has been able to say for sure how it got there. They know she died when she was thirty-five years old, that her remains are 2,000 years old, and that she was mummified at a time when practitioners were getting a little sloppy about the process, but all Cynthia knows about her recent history is that the museum and the mummy have both been there since 1956. Nobody knows where the mummy came from before that. Cynthia said, "A lot of the people involved are still alive, but not all of them remember where the trucking company went to get things. One woman who might know has long since moved, and we can't find her."

The best rumor about the mummy is that another museum rejected it because it was cursed. Maybe it was a good curse. Good things certainly have been happening while Ms. Mummy lives at the Arts and Science Center. Open Tuesday through Saturday from 11:30 A.M. to 5:00 P.M. and Sunday from 2:00 to 5:00 P.M. Closed Monday. Free admission.

A POCKET OF HISTORY

Now head east on Highway 70 for twenty or thirty minutes to ◈ **Historic Salisbury.** Two kinds of people live here—those whose families have been in place for generations and those who have moved in recently, mostly from up north. Both share an almost smug conviction that theirs is one of the most congenial, historically interesting communities in North Carolina. I say *almost* smug because they're right. Although this is one of the oldest towns in the area, and the entire 23-block downtown community of commercial and residential buildings dating from 1820 to 1920 is on the National Register of Historic Places, it receives relatively little attention from outside. The Historic Salisbury Foundation and an active group of supporters are trying to change that.

They point to the 1898 Grimes Mill, a roller mill with all its original machinery in five floors; the Civil War Salisbury Confederate Prison Site and National Cemetery, where the largest number of unknown Civil War soldiers are buried; and the restored Railroad Depot. All of them are open to the public.

Then there's the Historic Salisbury walking tour that includes the homes in the National Register Historic District. Some of these homes are open to the public. The ◈ **Dr. Josephus Hall House,** 226 South Jackson Street, for instance, is a large, 1820 antebellum house that sits among old oaks and boxwoods that have been in place nearly as long as the house. Dr. Hall was chief surgeon at the Salisbury Confederate Prison during the Civil War. After the war, the Union commander used the house as headquarters. Somehow the grounds and the interior escaped the destruction typically associated with Yankee occupation in the South, and the Hall House contains nearly all its original furnishings. Open Saturday and Sunday from 2:00 to 5:00 P.M. Modest admission fee (704–636–0103).

Also on Jackson Street, the ◈ **Rowan Museum,** in the 1819 Judge James Martin House, has hand-carved Stirewalt house mantels, magnificent woodwork and trim, and a spiral staircase that curves up for three floors to an impressive ceiling medallion. The museum contains collections of early Rowan County history and several rooms furnished in the style of the period with work by Rowan craftsmen. Open Thursday through Sunday from 2:00 to 5:00 P.M. Closed legal holidays. A modest admission fee is charged (704–633–5946).

Moving from the historic to the contemporary, the ❖ **Water-works Visual Arts Center,** at the corner of West Kerr and Water streets, features changing exhibits of contemporary art. The outdoor sculpture garden is especially pleasant on clear, sunny days. The gallery is in a building that was first used as the Salisbury Waterworks and then as the city police station. Its large open spaces are especially suited to displaying art. Open Tuesday through Friday from 10:00 A.M. to 5:00 P.M.; Saturday from 9:00 A.M. to 4:00 P.M.; and Sunday from 1:00 to 4:00 P.M. Closed Mondays. Nominal donations are suggested.

In downtown Salisbury, which you really must see for its remarkable old factory, old train station (where Amtrak now stops), and business buildings, you can break the fast-food habit by having a bite of lunch at **Spanky's,** an old-fashioned ice-cream parlor that serves not only homemade ice-cream concoctions, but also good soups, salads, deli sandwiches, and cheesecake (704–638–0780). Spanky's actually makes seventy-five different flavors of ice cream, but the owner explained, almost apologetically, that they keep only twenty-five flavors on hand at a time! The restaurant is in an old building that in 1859 was the tallest in North Carolina. Open Monday through Saturday from 9:00 A.M. to 8:00 P.M., and Sunday from noon to 8:00 P.M.

When you're ready to spend the night, ❖ **Rowan Oak House,** 208 Fulton Street offers Victorian elegance in a 1902 Queen Anne house (704–633–2086). The house is notable for its remarkably intact interior, where the original wallpaper is still in perfect condition.

When you're ready to leave Salisbury, take Highway 52 South for an interesting drive that shows you the down-home, not the tourist, version of the Piedmont. In about 6 miles, almost before you've left Salisbury's environs, you come to Granite Quarry, where a big billboard on the left side of the road directs you to ❖ **Kluttz Piano Factory.** They deliver free, but probably not if you live in Cincinnati. Stop in and look around, even though you probably aren't looking to buy a piano while you're out tracking unbeaten paths. This place, which advertises over 500 new and rebuilt pianos, is awesome. The showroom, where you try out new and reconditioned pianos, looks fairly standard, but you'll be dumbfounded by the work area that seems roughly the size of a football field, filled with pianos—whole pianos and pieces of pianos in every make, model, and size. Ten minutes of just looking will tell you more about what's inside a piano than you've ever dreamed you could know. The people who work here talk as casually about the good and bad traits of grands, uprights, spinets, Yamahas, Wurlitzers, and Baldwins as the rest of us talk about the tomatoes in our gardens.

Outsiders sometimes get a chuckle out of the name *Kluttz,* but around here, Kluttz is just another family name, belonging not only to the owners of the piano factory, but also to architects, contractors, and art shop proprietors. Everybody works hard, even the older Mr. Kluttz, who thinks nothing of being one of two men to haul a grand piano off its legs, out of a truck, and into a house. You'll notice some of the people wear big gold belt buckles shaped like grand pianos. Ask about the buckles, and the only answer you'll get is, "It means we're special." Some workers get there as early as 4:00 A.M., but regular hours for ordinary mortals are Monday through Friday from 8:00 A.M. to 5:00 P.M. and Saturday from 8:00 A.M. to 3:00 P.M. (704–279–7237).

Continuing on Highway 52 South, which is really going east at this point, brings you to ❖ **Rockwell,** which you should pronounce *ROCKwul,* not *RockWELL.* The town bears no relationship to Norman Rockwell, but it should: Flags fly from all the porches on Memorial Day; signs advertise "bait, crickets and night crawlers"; women still appear occasionally with their hair in curlers; neighbors stop each other in the grocery store to ask if the new "granbaby" has arrived yet; pink and blue bows on mailboxes announce when the new grans do come into the world. Stop for some good, authentic barbecue at ❖ **Darrell's Bar-BQ** in Rockwell. If you call ahead, you can even pick it up at a drive-through window, although then you'll miss the chance to mingle with the local people inside (704–279–6300). Darrell's is open Tuesday through Saturday from 10:00 A.M. to 9:00 P.M. Closed Sunday and Monday.

Back on Highway 52 and driving southeast again, you'll pass a couple of permanent yard-sale junk shops, a tattoo shop, a few roadside taverns, and lots of modest country homes, some in dreadful disarray and some perfectly kept, with geraniums and picket fences. About 10 miles beyond Rockwell, you'll come to P. J.'s Place, a gas stop and beer store. Inside you can almost always find a few folks sitting around sipping Miller Lite or Budweiser—the local preferences— and gossiping or playing cards. You can have a beer on the spot or buy a six to take out.

Whether you stop or not, use this landmark to find the turn from Highway 52 onto Old Beatty Ford Road for an hour's diversion down a rural entrepreneurial row. The best way to be sure you don't miss it is to drive to P. J.'s, turn around and backtrack a few seconds to where you'll see the Old Beatty Ford sign, and turn left onto a road that crosses the railroad tracks and runs past a large quarry operation. You'll drive about 12 miles along this road, past a Soil Conservation Service demonstration farm on the left, a home-based sewing machine repair shop called Sew and Sew, another home business, "Why Knot Upholstery," and Miller Farms Racing (a track around grassy fields). Among these little businesses, many yards have for-sale signs offering produce in season, a piece of used farm equipment, a boat, a camper "like new" with tow bar and a pickup (there must be a story in that one), firewood, oil paintings—it all changes with fortune and the seasons. You'll also pass a couple of uncommonly attractive older churches, the kind with their own manicured graveyards in back. Old Concord Road intersects Old Beatty Ford Road after about 12 miles. Turn left. Drive about 3 miles more, passing Roy Cline Road and Irish Potato Road to turn right immediately onto Goldfish Road. You're at ❖ **Greendale,** which from the outside looks like one more sprawling roadside building. Inside you'll find wonder and the ultimate rural entrepreneurial enterprise.

Long rows of beautifully clear, brightly lighted aquariums gleam in the dim room. Here in the boonies, where if you tell your mother you're going to the fish store she assumes you're going to buy flounder, you discover gouramis and guppies, oscars, cichlids, corals, and saltwater exotics whose names you don't even know, all apparently thriving. OK, you can't keep goldfish on the road, but just the looking beats watching television, and you may find the selection and prices on aquarium equipment appealing enough to tease a traveler's check out of your wallet before you leave.

Greendale started out as a goldfish farm back in 1929, when Rufus Green got laid off by Cannon Mills and decided to make his living raising goldfish in outdoor ponds to sell to dime stores. One of his first sales was to get money to buy a shirt for church. As years passed, Rufus died, and his wife maintained the business as well as she could. Rufus's son, George, returned in 1978 from another war that wasn't called one, with his wife, Gaysorn, a classical dancer from Bangkok. By now hobbyists had turned enthusiastically to exotic tropical fish, so it made sense for Greendale to develop accordingly. The whole story, in a yellowing newspaper clipping, is taped to the front wall.

It's hard to imagine there would be enough customers to keep the business going, but they come from all directions: Concord, Kannapolis, Salisbury, Albemarle. The store is closed on Tuesdays, partly because new shipments of plants and fish come then. On Wednesdays it's so busy that, as one employee put it, "People just come in and throw money at you." They're all there, Gay and George, Mrs. Rufus Green, and local young people who work here and often get themselves hooked on the hobby in the process. You can always find someone to chat with about the troublesome habits of live bearers and how hard it is not to disrupt a gourami's bubble nest (704–933–1798). Open Monday and Wednesday through Saturday from 10:00 A.M. to 6:00 P.M. and Sunday from 2:00 to 6:00 P.M. Closed Tuesday.

When you leave, depending on which way you turn, you may see a large block-lettered sign inside a cul-de-sac in front of a mobile home: IF YOU DON'T HAVE BUSINESS HERE, THIS IS A GOOD PLACE FOR YOU TO TURN AROUND. This may be the only guy in the county who isn't looking for customers at home. The best way to return to Highway 52 is the way you came in. Since everything looks different going in the opposite direction, you'll see things you missed the first time and won't feel that you're backtracking.

Coming into Misenhiemer, Highway 52 runs through the middle of the small **Pfeiffer College** campus, where all the classroom buildings, administration buildings, dormitories, and faculty houses are made of red brick. You might think that this is the kind of place a film director would like to shoot *Who's Afraid of Virginia Woolf?*, although a director would never get approval in this Bible pocket. If it did happen, people would raise a big stink in the *Stanley News and Press*.

FARM COUNTRY

From Pfeiffer College it's only a couple of miles to the intersection of Highway 52 and Highway 49 at Richfield. Go north on Highway 49 for about as long as you need to take two deep breaths and pull into the parking lot of the ◆**Motel Restaurant.** This is the breakfast and lunch spot for many of the local farmers, the people who work in the mobile home factories and the Perfect Fit textile plant down the road. For breakfast you get two eggs, bacon, grits or hash browns, biscuits or cornbread, and coffee for about $2.50. Lunch is one meat (meatloaf or fried fish, maybe; the selections are written on a blackboard at the door), two vegetables, and beverage for $3.75. Sit at the counter and you can study the ever-lengthening row of imprinted mugs: *Old Age Ain't No Place for Sissies, If God Wanted Me to Cook and Clean My Hands Would've Been Made of Aluminum, My Parents Went to Myrtle Beach and All They Got Me Was This Dumb Mug, God Loves You and I'm Trying.*

The Motel Restaurant waitresses know all the regulars by name, ask, "You doin' OK?" as they take your order, and after the first time, remember what it is that you always have. They like a good joke. Did you hear about the prostitute who told her tax consultant that she was a chicken farmer? Well, she said . . . Country music plays in the background, and while Willie and Waylon are appreciated, one of the waitresses says she'd really like to marry Conway, even if she is already married and he's old. But Randy Travis, now, he's one of our own, coming from Monroe and all. When you've had all the coffee or iced tea you can hold, leave a couple quarters on the counter, pay your bill, and when someone says, "Come back," you say, "I'll do it." Open Monday through Friday from 5:00 A.M. to 2:00 P.M. and Saturday from 5:00 to 11:00 A.M.

From here you could take Highway 49 North through the Uhwarrie Forest back up to Asheboro, or you could go south for an interesting drive to Charlotte. Expect to have to be patient. The road is only one lane in each direction, with few places to pass, and you'll probably spend some time behind a tractor or a slow-moving truck hauling logs. Even going slowly, you'll be at Mount Pleasant in ten or fifteen minutes.

Shortly before you come to the crossroads at Mount Pleasant, a sign on the right advertises ❖ **Cline's Country Antiques.** A big, rusting antique tractor marks the lane back to the seven long buildings where Don Cline manages an ever-changing stock. He buys and wholesales antiques by the truckload but attends with equal care to your $5 purchase of an old advertising sign or kitchen utensil. One of the most fascinating things you can do is ask for a particular kind of antique—an oak washstand or armoire, or a pie safe, for instance—and then watch Don reflect a minute before he directs you, without consulting any kind of inventory list at all, to the precise building and corner in which you'll find what you're looking for. No one's quite sure how he does it, but no matter how often or how fast his inventory changes, Don always knows where everything is.

His appearance reflects the fact that Don detests malls and spending money on glitzy new things; he prides himself on living out of his junk. His britches came from a load the pickers hauled in, his sweater was in a bin of post office surplus that he found at a dumpster, and his Sunday suit was part of the stock he got when he bought all the remaining merchandise of a department store that went out of business several years ago.

If he's not out supervising the coming and going of truckloads, Don will probably be sitting in the old barber chair by the wood stove in the barn talking with visiting dealers or reading old issues of antiques magazines. A couple of years ago, Don collaborated with a professional writer on the book, *Buying and Selling Antiques*. Across from Don's barber chair, Vichard, his assistant, nailed up a wooden box to hold copies of the book, with a sign above that reads THE BOOK and an arrow pointing down to the copies that are for sale.

The idea of Don's writing a book seems surprising when you first encounter his plain-old-country-boy demeanor, but pay attention, ask a few questions, and you'll learn that he has taught economics in a couple of area colleges, has a photographic memory, and is perfectly willing to let you think he's stupid if you're so inclined because it helps business. Not that he's dishonest; he won't sell an imperfect piece without pointing out the flaw, he won't knowingly misrepresent anything, and he charges only a modest markup on his merchandise. Don Cline may be the most scrupulously honest antiques dealer in the business, but he doesn't see any reason to rouse your jousting instincts by flaunting his brain.

Actually, in the beginning he wasn't that eager to go into business at all. It's just that he loved auctions and couldn't resist good buys. When he got married, his wife pointed out that unless he started moving stuff out at something close to the speed with which he brought it in, there wasn't going to be room for her. Then too, there on his father's farm were all those long chicken sheds, empty since the cholesterol scare made producing eggs unprofitable. All the setup really needed was customers, so Don began to let it be known that he had some stuff to sell. The rest, as they say, is history. Cline's Country Antiques (704–436–6824) is open from sometime around 8:00 or 9:00 A.M. to sometime about dark, Tuesday through Saturday. Closed Sunday and Monday.

If you get to hanging around the Cline place so late you don't feel like driving anymore, you could stay at the **Carolina Country Inn** in Mount Pleasant. This is a simple, clean, quiet motel, with a sign out front pointing out how many long country miles you still have to Charlotte or Raleigh and inviting you to stay there instead. A few rooms have refrigerators. Rates are modest (704–436–9616).

When you get to where Highway 601 meets Highway 49, you may decide to make a side trip on Highway 601 South to Highway 200 and follow the signs to the ❖ **Reed Gold Mine** at Stanfield, about 10 miles east of Concord (704–786–8337). This is the site of the first authenticated gold find in the United States. It seems that Conrad Reed found a gold nugget the size of a brick on his farm and after that sort of lost interest in farming. We tend to associate the gold rushes with Alaska and California, but the fever burned here in North Carolina back in the late 1820s. For a time more people worked at gold mining than any other occupation except farming. Here and there in the state you still find places such as Morning Star Explorations at Richfield where the search for more gold continues or has begun anew. At the Reed Gold Mine State Historic Site, you can pan for gold in the spring and summer and tour the mining area year-round. In the visitors center, exhibits and a film explain the history and mining process. Admission is free, but a modest fee is charged for panning. Open April 1 to October 31, Monday through Saturday from 9:00 A.M. to 5:00 P.M. and Sunday from 1:00 to 5:00 P.M. Open November 1 through March 31, Tuesday through Saturday from 10:00 A.M. to 4:00 P.M. and Sunday from 1:00 to 4:00 P.M. Closed Monday.

LAND OF THE NEW

Charlotte's an exciting place to visit these days. It's growing so fast that you can find something new almost every day, and everybody is feeling upbeat and turned on about it. People seem to exude civic pride. Because they're so pleased about the way things are going, they're incredibly nice to visitors. Charlotte has reason for pride: a National Basketball Association expansion team, the Charlotte Hornets; the Carolina Panthers NFL football team; the Charlotte Knights professional baseball team; NASCAR racing at Charlotte Motor Speedway; Douglas International Airport, with direct flights to major cities; a Pulitzer Prize–winning newspaper, the *Charlotte Observer;* the highly rated University of North Carolina at Charlotte; a slew of smaller colleges and universities; new skyscrapers; and a new coliseum and an old coliseum.

Until Hurricane Hugo hit in the fall of 1989, Charlotte was famous for its streets lined with huge old oak trees. People called the city "The Shady Lady." Since the 90-mile-per-hour winds, things are a lot more open—including some roofs—but even before the repairs were finished, committees were planting new trees and Charlottians were looking proudly at the neighborliness and cooperation with which they handled the days- and weeks-long power outage and the physical destruction to homes, neighborhoods, and businesses. That fighting spirit, they'll tell you, has always been part of the city's heritage.

Originally the city was named for Queen Charlotte of Mecklenburg, wife of King George III, and it still calls itself "The Queen City," but the city rebelled against England in 1775 and earned from General Cornwallis the complaint that Charlotte was "a hornet's nest." That historical epithet figured in naming the new NBA team the Hornets.

Charlotte's growth brings traffic, unfortunately, along with the excitement, but it would be too bad to miss some of the city's special features because of traffic. The best advice for a visitor to minimize problems is to study a city map ahead of time and try to avoid the major high-traffic highways—Interstates 85 and 77 and Independence Boulevard—as much as possible. Once you're actually in the city, the traffic isn't bad, except at rush hour; it's the main arteries that clog up. Don't hesitate to ask for directions if you get confused. People seem to be used to it and are good at helping, probably because the ongoing construction everywhere has forced them to figure out new routes.

You'll find enough special places here to warrant spending a night, so perhaps you'll want to arrange for accommodations first. In addition to plenty of standard hotels and motels, Charlotte has an exceptionally pleasant and successful bed-and-breakfast inn, the Inn on Providence, 6700 Providence Road.

At ◆**The Homeplace** (704–365–1936), Frank and Peggy

Dearien bought a restored country Victorian home with the requisite heart-of-pine floors, formal parlor, and 10-foot beaded ceilings. The next thing anyone knew, they were operating a bed-and-breakfast inn, serving bountiful breakfasts, and as a bit of *lagniappe,* evening desserts. The house is decorated in a soothing combination of blue and rose colors. A unique aspect of the decor is the collection of primitive paintings, painted over the past ten or so years by John Gentry, Peggy's father, with his handwritten stories on the back personalizing each one. This inn has become very popular with business travelers, so it's always busy. You will need to make a reservation well ahead of time to stay here.

The ✦**Mint Museum of Art,** at 2730 Randolph Road, has exhibits that celebrate both local history and world culture. The name comes from the building's having been a branch of the United States Mint in the 1800s. That made sense back when the Piedmont was producing most of the country's gold.

In 1988 the museum created a huge stir with the exhibit, "Ramses the Great: the Pharaoh and His Time," which featured, among other items, a gold statue of the pharaoh so large the building had to be modified to give him extra headroom. That exhibit is gone now, but a new permanent collection, "Spanish Colonial Art," is attracting attention. Other permanent collections include American and European paintings, African artifacts, pre-Columbian arts, costumes, and gold and currency of the Carolinas.

The Mint Museum Gift Shop specializes in offerings that reflect the museum exhibits. For instance, in connection with the pre-Columbian art exhibit, the shop sells replicas of pre-Columbian gold charms. Artifacts imported directly from African suppliers complement the museum's African displays. As the exhibits change, so do some of the gifts. A standard item in the shop that makes a nice gift is the miniature brass replica of Queen Charlotte's gold crown. A painting in which she wears the original crown hangs in a prominent position. The museum is open Tuesday from 10:00 A.M. to 10:00 P.M.; Wednesday through Saturday from 10:00 A.M. to 5:00 P.M.; and Sunday from 1:00 to 6:00 P.M. Closed Monday. Also closed Christmas and New Year's Day. Modest admission charged but free to all Tuesdays from 5:00 to 10:00 P.M. and the second Sunday of each month (704–337–2000).

Another museum in the vicinity worth your attention is the ✦**Hezekiah Alexander Homesite** and Museum of History, at

The Hezekiah Alexander Homesite

3500 Shamrock Drive (704–568–1774). The Hezekiah Alexander house is the oldest dwelling still standing in Mecklenburg County. It was built of local quarry stone in 1774 and has been restored. Costumed guides lead tours of the house, log kitchen, barn, and gardens. The history museum displays local crafts and artifacts. Hezekiah was a delegate to the Fifth Provincial Congress and served on the committee that drafted the North Carolina State Constitution and Bill of Rights. The site has a number of fascinating details. The house is known as "The Rockhouse." Its doors are unusually low by today's standards, a feature intended to keep heat inside when people opened the doors. In the master bedroom, a rope bed dominates the room. This is the kind of bed in which a latticework of ropes supported the mattress. Every so often the ropes had to be tightened—giving rise to the old phrase, "sleep tight." Don't even think about the origins of the rest of the phrase saying, "Don't let the bedbugs bite." The boys' rooms on the back side of the house also served as an army post during the Revolutionary War. And in the recreated spring house behind the house, you see how milk and butter were cooled in the late 1700s. Admission to the museum is free; a modest fee is charged for tours. Open Tuesday through Friday from 10:00 A.M. to 5:00 P.M., and Saturday and Sunday from 2:00 to 5:00 P.M.

In uptown Charlotte at 301 North Tryon Street, the kids will enjoy ◆ **Discovery Place,** a hands-on science and technology museum where they can enjoy some close-up experiences with fish and birds, the natural sciences, and computers (704–372–6261). One of the most impressive exhibits is the tropical rain forest, which fills three stories with plants, rocks, waterfalls, and appropriate wildlife. The exhibits related to the human body are interesting, too. One description claims that you learn about characteristics of the human body in a "hands-on manner," which could make you nervous if you didn't know about models and machines. Open weekdays from 9:00 A.M. to 5:00 P.M.; Saturday from 9:00 A.M. to 6:00 P.M.; and Sunday from 1:00 to 6:00 P.M. A moderate admission is charged.

When you need nourishment, you have a surprisingly varied choice, especially when you consider that only a decade or so ago your choices were southern homestyle and southern homestyle plus a Greek restaurant with food remarkably similar to southern homestyle. In the uptown area, **Carpe Diem,** 431 South Tryon Street, offers a variety of "new American" entrees, including vegetarian dishes, reflecting some Middle Eastern and Caribbean influences. The restaurant serves lunch and dinner. Phone (704) 377-7976. Also in the uptown area, **Ginger Root**, 201 East Fifth Street, serves gourmet Chinese food for lunch and dinner. The restaurant is on the first floor of the Apparel Center. Phone (704) 377-9429. But one of the most interesting restaurants is ◆**The Pewter Rose,** at 1820 South Boulevard, close to the southeast edge of town and not difficult to reach (704-332-8149). Helen Scruggs had a small luncheon restaurant of the same name at Spirit Square in uptown Charlotte. Before opening the new and improved restaurant, she studied the culinary arts in France and then duplicated the feel with a cozy French country decor in the new Pewter Rose, in a renovated textile mill. You'll feel comfortable here in either informal or business dress, and you'll find menu items ranging from fancy burgers to some outstanding salads and platters. The smoked turkey with béarnaise mayonnaise on orange nut bread is worth several trips across town. All the desserts, which you can order for lunch or dinner or in the bar, are homemade. You'll like the price range, too, roughly $5.00 to $15.00. Open for lunch Monday through Saturday from 11:00 A.M. to 2:00 P.M. and Sunday from 11:00 A.M. to 3:00 P.M.; for dinner Monday through Thursday from 5:00 to 10:00 P.M., Friday and Saturday from 5:00 to 11:00 P.M., and Sunday from 5:00 to 9:00 P.M.

Another place that's easy to find is ◆**Dilworth Brewing Company** (704-377-2739), 1301 East Boulevard, where the salad, steak, and chicken menu is accompanied by a choice of several beers, porter, and ale from the microbrewery. You can see the steel workings of the brewery from the dining area. Classic French onion soup and chili are on the menu every day, along with a soup du jour. You can also order a variety of trendy snacks: nachos, buffalo wings, raw veggies, and a great beer-batter onion loaf. The Dilworth Brewing Company is very popular for lunch among people who work in the vicinity, so you might like to time your own repast to fall a little before or after the traditional noon lunch hour. Open Monday through Thursday from 11:00 A.M. to midnight and Friday and Saturday from 11:00 A.M. to 1:00 A.M.

Charlotte has another brewpub, **Southend Brewery and Smokehouse**, at 2100 South Boulevard in the Atherton Mill Complex. This is a large establishment with the brewing vessels, enclosed in a glassed-in room, serving as the visual centerpiece of the space. The kitchen is also fully visible. The food is California style but also includes a number of smoked specialties, including ribs and sausages. They serve astonishingly large servings. One of the principals in this operation is said to have "invented" Bud Lite. Phone (704) 358–3424.

On the north side of Charlotte, on Highway 49, the botanical gardens at the University of North Carolina/Charlotte deserve a lot more attention than they receive. The gardens have three parts, the McMillan Greenhouse, the VanLandingham Glen, and the Susie Harwood Garden. The greenhouse has one of the best collections of tropical orchids in the south, with something like 800 species. The tropical rainforest coservatory is a convincing simulation of a real rain forest. Other greenhouse rooms include a cactus room and a cool room. The VanLandingham Glen started as a rhododendron garden in 1966 and has expanded to include more than 4,000 rhododendrons, mostly hybrids. Another interesting feature is the 1,000 species of Carolina-native plants growing in the gardens. The Hardwood garden, with gravel paths is more formal and and includes exotic plants from around the world. The collection of Japanese maples is noteworthy, as is the winter garden. The greenhouse is open during normal business hours but you can visit the gardens any time. Because construction on campus will affect traffic patterns for the foreseeable future, the best way to find the gardens is to go onto campus through the main gate on Highway 49 and follow the signs to the visitor parking garage and ask for directions from there. For more information call the university's main switchboard a (704) 547–2000.

About 20 miles west of Charlotte, in Gastonia, which you can reach quickly on Interstate 85, the ◆ **Schiele Museum of Natural History and Planetarium** attracts large numbers of visitors, especially schoolchildren, with its collection of North American mammals in habitat settings, a 100-seat planetarium, a restored pioneer site of the 1700s, and a Catawba Indian village. Other exhibits deal with everything from forestry to archaeology. A brochure maps out several self-guided tour suggestions for the outside grounds. Don't skip this one because it's popular; it has good reason for being so. Open Tuesday through Friday from 9:00 A.M. to 5:00 P.M. and Saturday and Sunday from 2:00 to 5:00 P.M. Planetarium shows offered only Saturday and Sunday afternoon. Admission free (704–864–3962).

THE MOUNTAINS

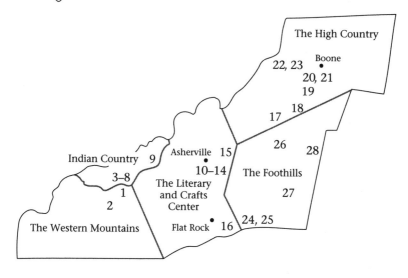

The High Country

Boone
22, 23 •
20, 21
19
18
17
26   28

Indian Country 9 Asherville 15
3–8   •
        10–14   The Foothills
1
            27
2

The Literary
and Crafts
Center

The Western Mountains   Flat Rock 16 24, 25
                            •

1. Randolph House
2. Nantahala Outdoor Center
3. Qualla Boundary Cherokee
   Indian Reservation
4. *Unto These Hills*
5. Cherokee Cyclorama Wax
   Museum
6. Oconaluftee Indian Village
7. Qualla Arts and Crafts
   Mutual, Inc.
8. Museum of the Cherokee
   Indian
9. Waynesville
10. Folk Art Center
11. Grove Park Inn
12. Biltmore Estate
13. Cedar Crest

14. Thomas Wolfe Memorial
15. Zebulon B. Vance Birthplace
16. Carl Sandburg Home
    National Historic Site
17. Mount Mitchell State Park
18. Linville Caverns
19. Grandfather Mountain
20. Blowing Rock
21. Tweetsie Railroad
22. Mast Store
23. Mast Farm Inn
24. Lake Lure
25. Lodge on Lake Lure
26. Song of the Wood
27. Casar
28. Carrigan Farms

THE MOUNTAINS

THE WESTERN MOUNTAINS

Whatever you plan in the North Carolina mountains, allow about twice as much travel time as usual. Narrow roads wind through woodland and countryside, up hills so steep you sometimes feel as though your car will peel off the road backward, from hairpin turns into switchbacks followed by more curves. The squiggles don't all show on the maps, and the maps can't allow for the time it takes if you get behind a big truck with no place to pass for 50 miles. Decide ahead of time not to hurry; relax and absorb the peerless scenery.

One way to enjoy the panoramic views of mountains and valleys is by driving some part of the Blue Ridge Parkway. It stretches from Shenandoah National Park along the Blue Ridge Mountains into the southern part of the Black Mountains, through the Craggies, the Pisgahs, the Balsams, and into the Great Smokies, a total of 469 miles. The maximum speed limit along the parkway is 45 miles per hour, but in reality, traffic is often slower. It doesn't take much arithmetic to figure that it would take a long time to cover the entire length of the parkway at 30 or 40 miles per hour. The best way to plan a trip is to alternate stretches of the parkway with drives on the roads you can reach by turning off along the way. Crossovers from the parkway are marked with mileposts that are numbered and named.

Before you get on the parkway, spend some time enjoying the Nantahala National Forest, Nantahala Gorge, and Bryson City in the mountains. In Bryson City, ◈**Randolph House,** built in 1895 by Amos Frye, is run today by his niece, Ruth Adams, and her husband, Bill, as a homey country inn. As Ruth tells it, Amos once had owned all the timber around, but when the government decided to declare most of the area national forestland, Amos had to sell. He kept the right to lumber out the sold acreage for a limited time; to get his money's worth, he set to building, using wood, of course, as fast as he could. Randolph House was one of the results.

Because the house is furnished with family antiques that have always been there, things don't all match, leaving you with the feeling that if you blink hard you'll see old Amos there in the worn leather chair. The inn's dinners are strictly by reservation because Ruth hates waste, and when you make the reservation, you choose from a list of entrees planned for that night. The cuisine might be called "Southern Gourmet," featuring choices such as Cornish hen in orange sauce and trout in pecan sauce, served perhaps with a classic southern squash casserole and a dessert of Three Hundred Dollar Chocolate Cake or Mile High Lemon Pie. Bill maintains a nice wine list. The inn is open April through October (704–488–3472).

From Bryson City, drive 9 miles southwest on Highway 19 to ◆ **Nantahala Outdoor Center** at the Nantahala Gorge. The outdoor center attracts the outdoors crowd, especially rafters and hikers. This is a congenial place to hire a guide and all the equipment you need for a white-water rafting trip down the Nantahala River. It's also great for fishing, picnicking, and hiking. Part of the fun is watching the serious rafters, who, as one observer put it, seem to have a continuing contest to see who can show up in the most worn, mismatched, clothes-don't-matter outfit. The Nantahala Outdoor Center Restaurant, right by the river, has been a popular eating place with hikers and rafters for years. Some of the most popular recipes have been bound into a cookbook, *River Runners Special,* with each recipe listed for difficulty (Class I, II, III, and so on) like the rapids on the river. Vegetarian lentil mushroom soup is Class II; amaretto cream pie is Class IV. In a recent change, the restaurant's name became River's End, to note the addition of another restaurant, Relia's Garden, at the center.

At River's End, you feel perfectly comfortable in your mismatched hiking clothes and down vest, sitting at a rustic table looking out over the river while you gobble a hearty serving of spicy beef stew with the restaurant's special herb bread. Relia's Garden is also casual, but a bit more upscale in its atmosphere and offerings. With a view of the mountains rather than the river, this restaurant sits in a field on the hill across the garden, landscaped with terraced gardens of herbs, unusual vegetables, and exotic plants. A walk through the gardens crushes fragrant bits of mint and thyme underfoot, so that no matter how hungry you were to begin with, your appetite's whetted even more by the time you go inside. Entrees range from fettuccine to prime rib. The county is dry, but brown bagging beer and wine are permitted.

Staff members of the Nantahala Outdoor Center, from guides to cooks, tend to return year after year, as do visitors. Moreover, the presence of the family that started the center is still much in evidence. Relia's Garden, for instance, is named for Arelia, wife of the founder and for many years director of food service. Her plants fill the terrace gardens. Spending time here feels like being part of an extended family or a close community. It is special. The center and restaurants operate from roughly mid-March to November 1, depending on the weather. River's End is open daily from 7:00 A.M. to 9:00 P.M. Relia's Garden serves breakfast daily from 8:00 to 10:30 A.M., lunch from 11:00 A.M. to 2:00 P.M., and dinner from 5:00 to 9:00 P.M. (10:00 P.M. Saturday). In the colder months, hours may be cut back. For information about the time you plan to be here, phone (704) 488–2175.

Just a few miles (a long walk or a short ride) beyond the outdoor center, Nantahala Village offers a less strenuous and very agreeable alternative approach to the river, the gorge, and the forest. Built before the white-water craze as a rustic resort in the woods, Nantahala Village has simple rooms in the inn and a variety of cozy cabins built of logs or native stone, with knotty pine interiors. The cabins have kitchens; some have fireplaces.

The dining room in the inn serves an interesting combination of traditional foods—chicken, beef, and so on—as well as popular entrees lower in fat and emphasizing the flavors of fresh herbs. John Burton and Jan Letendre are owners who have committed to keeping the original atmosphere and setting but wanted to update the dining room menu to include vegetarian and lighter fare. They offer these options along with the traditional southern mountain favorites. They're also committed to getting people into appropriate accommodations. For instance, they wouldn't put a family with tiny children into a cabin that has a deck jutting out over a cliff or an elderly person into a room that requires a lot of walking to reach. Nantahala Village is usually open except for a few weeks in winter, but weather could change this. It's a good idea to call ahead (704–488–2826 or outside North Carolina 800–438–1507).

INDIAN COUNTRY

Picking up the Blue Ridge Parkway at Cherokee brings you to some decisions about the kind of tourist you mean to be. The town, in the ◆ **Qualla Boundary Cherokee Indian Reservation** where Highways 441 and 19 meet, maintains several features dedicated to preserving and explaining the history of the

Cherokee nation, which was nearly wiped out by the infamous "Trail of Tears" forced walk in 1838, when the U.S. government tried to relocate all Indians to west of the Mississippi River. Some of the Cherokees escaped the march by hiding in the hills.

Eventually they were able to return to this area where they were once the powerful Cherokee nation. Their story is told in ◈ *Unto These Hills,* an outdoor drama played by a cast of 130 people, beginning between 8:00 and 9:00 P.M. nightly, except Sunday, from mid-June through late August, in an outdoor theater that seats 2,800 people. The program is presented by the Cherokee Historical Association with support from the Theatre Arts Section of the North Carolina Arts Council and funds appropriated by the North Carolina General Assembly. The story begins with Spanish explorer Hernando DeSoto's arrival in 1540 and climaxes with the Trail of Tears exodus. Many of the players are descendants of the Cherokee who lived the story. Moderately high admission fee. Box office (704–497–2111) open from 9:00 A.M. to 10:00 P.M. during the summer season and from 9:00 A.M. to 4:30 P.M. in the off-season. The story and performances are frankly moving; it's not uncommon to see people in the audience cry.

Unfortunately, activities of this caliber are surrounded by the tourist-tacky pseudo-Indian concessions that seem to plague the areas around Indian populations across the country. Trying to sort out the authentic and the merely exploitative can be depressing. You can count on quality at the ◈ **Cherokee Cyclorama Wax Museum** and **Oconaluftee Indian Village,** which are also sponsored by the Cherokee Historical Association, where the Cherokee history has been told with life-sized dioramas, recorded narrations, and an electronic map. The Oconaluftee Indian Village, a living replication of a 1750s Cherokee village, shows you Indians practicing their historical crafts of basket making, pottery, canoe building, food preparations, and weaponry, and perhaps even more important, explaining the culture within which these activities proceeded. Hour-long tours begin every five minutes, but you are not locked into them, and there is plenty of time for exploring, photographing, and questioning. Open from 9:00 A.M. to 5:30 P.M., May through October. Moderately high admission charge (704–497–2111).

◈ **Qualla Arts and Crafts Mutual, Inc.,** the most successful Indian-owned and -operated craft cooperative in the country, at the entrance of the *Unto These Hills* theater on Highway

441, offers you an opportunity to buy genuine Indian beadwork, baskets, wood carvings, pots, masks, and the like. Cherokee work is displayed in separate rooms from that of other tribes. Open Monday through Saturday from 8:00 A.M. to 6:00 P.M. and Sunday from 8:00 A.M. to 5:00 P.M. These hours may vary slightly seasonally. It's a good idea to call ahead. (704–497–3103).

Finally, the ◆ **Museum of the Cherokee Indian** (704–497–3481) displays traditional arts and crafts and offers a video on the history of the nation, along with displays of tools and various accounts of the Trail of Tears journey. Open daily from 9:00 A.M. to 5:30 P.M., later during the summer. Modest admission charged. Closed Thanksgiving, Christmas, and New Year's Day. For full information about attractions, contact the Cherokee Travel Center (704–497–9195).

Cherokee is considered the gateway to the Great Smoky Mountains, and it seems important to mention, however briefly, the **Great Smoky Mountains National Park,** established in 1934 partly with money donated by John D. Rockefeller. The park merits a full book in itself: Elevations climb as you move along the northeast; plant life, wildlife, and scenery invite superlatives; the bears and the weather are unpredictable. About half the park falls in Tennessee, but North Carolinians, figuring there's plenty for all, forgive that. Staying on the North Carolina side, you'll find enough hiking, fishing, and camping to last most of your life without being repetitive. There are several visitors centers in the park. For information, call (616) 436–5615. It's a Tennessee number, but it's also park headquarters and the best place to start when you need advance information. The park is said to have attracted more than ten million visitors annually in recent years, mostly in the summer, although with about 500,000 acres to explore, there'd seem to be enough room for everyone. You'll probably enjoy your visit more if you avoid the peak summer season.

Your next major stop should probably be Asheville, altitude 2,250 feet, population just under 60,000. You can amble along the Blue Ridge Parkway to get there, or go more directly along Highway 19. Either way, you might detour onto Highway 23 to stop in ◆ **Waynesville** (you are now at altitude 3,000 feet), a little town of Scotch–Irish and English founding where travelers like to stop to get away from the obvious tourist attractions and enjoy some real people. Waynesville is the home of the annual ramps festival. The ramp is a rank, onionlike, wild plant of no particular virtue, except that every summer the people of Waynesville have a big party to cook it all the ways they can think of: steamed ramps, braised ramps, ramps à la king, ramps fritters. Presumably, somebody eats the results, but that is not as conspicuous as the cooking, which leaves a garlicky odor heavy on the town all day. For some reason, it's a popular time and place for politicians to appear. If you'd like to spend a night and have dinner in congenial, rustic surroundings here, try **Grandview Lodge,** owned and operated by Stanley and Linda Arnold (704–456–5212). The Arnolds are actually newcomers, escapees from corporate Chicago. The inn has been operating for the past fifty-plus years; the Arnolds took it over as part of a longtime dream in 1986. Linda's cooking, which emphasizes fresh produce and herbs, whole-grain flours, and homemade desserts, has been so popular that she published a cookbook, *The Grandview Lodge Cookbook,* for guests who hope to duplicate some of her meals at home. Stanley loves to play bridge: if you were to show up as a threesome looking for a fourth, you'd win his heart forever. Stan has another talent that fits interestingly into the Waynesville scene. He speaks Polish, Russian, German, and Hebrew. In recent years Waynesville has become known for international folk-dance festivals—which gives Stan a chance to try every language he knows.

Another place to eat in Waynesville is **Maggie's Galley III** (704–456–8945) at 22 Howell Mill Road. The building housing the restaurant was made from primitive log cabins. An earlier owner had an antiques business here, and as his need for space grew, he just kept tacking on additional old cabins. He used five cabins to make the building as it is today. Each of the cabins has a story and a bit of history attached. The restaurant has a flier with all the information. The food at the restaurant is gourmet quality, with fresh seafood, Black Angus steaks, and a few oddities such as alligator tail and a blackened bologna sandwich. The atmosphere is zany and a meal here, in addition to being good, is a lot of fun. Open daily from 11:30 A.M. to 9:30 P.M., Maggie's Galley is usually busy; reservations are a good idea.

The people who run this restaurant are friends with Donna and Gale Livengood, who have an equally zany and fun bed-and-breakfast inn, **Windsong** (704–627–6111) nearby at Clyde. Windsong is a contemporary rustic log home built especially as a

B&B by the Livengoods. It sits on the side of a mountain and the side looking over that vista is virtually all windows so that you have a glorious view from your room, the dining room, and the lower floor recreation room. The high, beamed ceilings and light pine wood throughout give the place a bright, light feeling. Each of the guest rooms has a private deck or patio outside and a huge soaking tub inside. The rooms are decorated thematically with furnishings the Livengoods have acquired mainly from the varied places their children have lived and worked. Hence, the Safari Room, with a toy giraffe peeking through the philodendrons by the soaking tub; the Alaska Room, with a real dogsled and Eskimo art; the Santa Fe Room, with a bed headboard of logs and rawhide; and the Country Room, with quilts and dried flowers. The full breakfast here is awesome.

Associated with Windsong B&B, Windsong Llama Treks, Ltd. provides a hiking possibility for which all you have to do is show up. The llamas, who live at Windsong, carry your pack; the people in charge pack your meals. Day treks, overnight treks, and longer treks are available. For overnighters you camp on the trail, but this kind of camping is pretty luxurious. You sleep two to a three-person-sized tent on the best inflatable trail mattresses. The food is not a hiker's usual dried mix fare but gourmet chicken, quality coffee, and chilled wines or mineral water, all possible because llamas can willingly pack more weight than people. Treks are available May through October. The trails are in some of the most secluded and beautiful wooded areas of the Smoky Mountains. The trek leaders are young and personable.

THE LITERARY AND CRAFTS CENTER

It's only 25 miles from Waynesville to Asheville. **Asheville** is crammed with arts, crafts, antiques, literary and musical people, and a healthy assortment of free spirits deeply involved in the unique Appalachian culture. The best place for variety and quality to see and buy area crafts is the ◆ **Folk Art Center,** just east of town at milepost 382 on the Blue Ridge Parkway, about a half mile north of Highway 70. It has been operated by the Southern Highland Handicraft Guild since 1980 and houses permanent and traveling exhibits and the Allanstand Craft Shop, where you can buy items similar to those in the exhibits. Crafts represented include weaving, pottery, basketry, quilting, jewelry, wood carving, stitchery, and musical instruments. Admission is free; donations are welcome. Open every day except Thanksgiving, Christmas, and New Year's Day from 9:00 A.M. to 5:00 P.M. Closed occasionally for inventory and changing exhibitions (704–298–7928).

At the edge of town, two well-known attractions here have become almost obligatory stops for anyone who wants to claim to have seen the area: Grove Park Inn and Biltmore Estate. Both nearly defy description. As newspaper writer Jean Thwaite once said of ❖**Grove Park Inn,** "It would almost be ugly, were it not so interesting." The building, of a size that seems to dwarf pyramids, is built of red boulders hauled from Sunset Mountain, on which it's located, in 1913. William Grove did well, to understate matters, in pharmaceuticals in St. Louis. He liked Asheville, so he bought a lot of it, including Sunset Mountain. Then eschewing architects, who didn't understand him, he got his son-in-law to design and build (without a contractor) the massive hotel. The inn is 500 feet long, with a flagstone-floored lobby 80 feet wide and almost half the length of a football field. The fireplaces at each end are so big they burn 12-foot logs, and when there's no fire, children can walk into them upright to play.

George Washington didn't sleep here, but practically everyone else of importance has: Thomas Edison, Henry Ford, Enrico Caruso, the Roosevelts, Dwight Eisenhower, even F. Scott Fitzgerald. Today the inn is popular with people looking for a place to celebrate a special occasion and with companies and organizations that want somewhere extra nice to gather their members.

After recent additions the inn has more than 500 rooms. Facilities include five restaurants, four cocktail lounges, indoor and outdoor swimming pools, golf, tennis, racquetball, a fitness center with aerobics room, weight room, Nautilus equipment, whirlpools, and saunas. The accommodations are luxurious; rates are correspondingly high, although they drop considerably in the off-season, when a variety of special packages are available (704–252–2711 or 800–438–5800).

Many of the packages include a tour of the ❖**Biltmore Estate,** which seems appropriate because it operates on the same grand scale. Like Mr. Grove, George Vanderbilt liked Asheville, and he too had a little money. He bought a lot of Asheville, too, about 125,000 acres, and had a 250-room private home built on the property. (Today only 7,500 acres belong to the estate. The

105

rest is part of the Blue Ridge Parkway or Mount Pisgah National Forest.) The home was famous from the beginning for its beauty of design and workmanship. The master builders were brought from Europe. The home was also famous for being ahead of its time in its modern conveniences, having early forerunners of washing machines and driers. Art in the mansion includes originals by Boldini, Ming dynasty china, and antiques that belonged to Napoleon.

It will take you the better part of a day to see the place properly, especially if you go beyond the mansion to explore the gardens and visit the winery. Although the Biltmore Estate Winery is still relatively young, some oenophiles say the wines—red, white, rosé, and champagne—are developing nicely. They are for sale, priced in the moderate range. Admission fees to the Biltmore Estate are high. The estate is open daily from 9:00 A.M. to 5:00 P.M. (704–255–1700 or 800–543–2961).

If you're not overwhelmed by the grandeur of Biltmore Estate, you're a rare bird. A nice way to decompress and get things back in perspective again is to spend a night at ◆ **Cedar Crest,** 674 Biltmore Avenue (704–252–1389). This bed-and-breakfast inn has

Biltmore Estate and Gardens

ten rooms in the main house and a guest cottage. There are a two-bedroom suite with a parlor and fireplace and a single-bedroom suite with a parlor. This is an 1890 Queen Anne–style Victorian mansion in which the work was purportedly done by the same craftsmen who worked on the Biltmore mansion. Apparently, once they were in this country and established in the little village built for them to work on Biltmore, they decided to hang around afterward and pick up a few odd jobs. Like the Biltmore Estate, Cedar Crest is so full of wonderful features that you can't take them all in at once, but the scale is more human and easier to relate to. The elaborate, first-generation oak wood-work differs in every room, with such subtle distinctions as being heavy and masculine in the library, but delicate and ornate in the dining room, which was considered a ladies' territory. Other special features in the house include a corner fireplace with fluted columns, a gilded cherub, and splendid stained-glass windows. There's a secret closet where silverware used to be hidden in troubled times. And the house has what may be the longest (6 feet) and smallest (4 feet) bathtubs in North Carolina. Jack McEwan will guide you through the splendors of the place with infectious enthusiasm. Then, to home in on the down-to-earth, creature-comfort level, you need to know about Barbara McEwan's "Victorian hanging garden," as she calls it. At Cedar Crest the bed sheets, after they are washed, are hung out on the clothesline to dry in the sun. If you've never slept inhaling the fragrance of line-dried sheets, you'll have to trust the word of those who have. It's the ultimate sensual delight.

Another place in Asheville worth a stop is the **Richmond Hill Inn** (87 Richmond Hill Drive; 704–252–7313; 800–545–9238), even if you aren't looking for overnight lodging. This is a luxurious inn with an heroic saved-from-the-wrecking-ball story. The century-old mansion was the home of a former congressman and diplomat, Richmond Pearson, and his wife, Gabrielle. It was one of the most innovative and elegant homes of its time. But it outlasted the people who wanted to live that way and could afford it. Toward the end, the Pearson's daughter, Marjorie, then an elderly woman, lived there alone, using just one room.

In subsequent sales and maneuvering, the building was scheduled to be torn down and then reprieved several times. Many community organizations, including the Preservation Society, campaigned and raised money to try to save the mansion. They also found the Michel family, who were willing to buy and restore it. It was moved, *all in one piece,* to its current spot on the hill. You can begin your stay here by watching a videotape showing the tense moving process.

The building was preserved where possible and restored or recreated where necessary, with fidelity to the mansion's original state. Much work was done by hand as it would originally have been rather than with electric tools. Now listed on the National Register of Historic Places, it is considered one of the best examples of a Queen Anne–style mansion. It's a must see if you are interested in architecture and preservation.

Because of the fine woodwork, soaring ceilings, and generously sized rooms, the mansion makes a fine inn. Some guest rooms are named for Pearson family members who once lived in them, others for important guests, and, on the third floor, for Asheville-connected writers, such as Carl Sandburg. Each writer's room has a picture of the writer and a collection of his or her books.

Also recreating the past, several hundred of Mr. Pearson's own books have been recovered and placed in the inn library along with books about North Carolina and those by North Carolina authors.

The restaurant is open to the public for dinner. It reflects the mansion's history in being named "Gabrielle's," after Mrs. Pearson. The food, however, is clearly a product of modern times. Considered American and nouvelle cuisine, it features lighter sauces and more healthful preparation than earlier haute cuisine.

Finding the place is tricky the first time. From Interstate 240 take the 19/23 Weaverville exit. Continue on 19/23 and turn at Exit 251 (UNC–Asheville). Turn left at the bottom of the ramp. At the first stoplight, turn left again onto Riverside Drive. Turn right on Pearson Bridge Road and cross the bridge. At the sharp curve, turn right on Richmond Hill Drive. The mansion is at the top of the hill.

An integral part of Asheville's intellectual and musical activity is **Malaprops Bookstore/Cafe,** 61 Haywood Street, where the ambience resembles what one imagines for Paris of the 1950s. Emoke Bracz, the owner, writes poetry. Other staff members produce fiction, nonfiction, and cartoons. North Carolina writers, of whom there are an astonishing number, stop in to browse or autograph, depending on their current state of productivity. In the background, music progresses through selections of jazz, New

Age, and folk, all of which you can buy in the downstairs cafe, where people sit around sipping coffee concoctions, nibbling desserts, and, presumably, talking either about their own writing or about the books upstairs. The offerings include many titles in poetry, feminist and women's books, and American Indian, travel, and North Carolina selections.

The unusual book stock and the unique atmosphere here made Malaprops something of a tourist attraction as well as a local center of the *literati*. Interestingly, the store is admired by many other bookstore proprietors and staff in the state. And although Malaprops likes paying customers as much as the next store, old school desks scattered about the place make for comfortable browsing, too (704–254–6734). Open Monday through Saturday from 9:00 A.M. to 8:00 P.M.; in July only, also open Sunday, noon to 5:00 P.M.

While you're feeling literary, visit the ◆ **Thomas Wolfe Memorial,** 48 Spring Street. This is the novelist's boyhood home, described in his novel, *Look Homeward, Angel,* as "Dixieland." In real life it was called "The Old Kentucky Home." Wolfe's mother, Julia, ran a boardinghouse in the rambling Victorian house, and its various rooms and furnishings, along with local people, were all incorporated into Wolfe's novel, mostly in unflattering terms. The people of Asheville didn't like that one bit, which led to Wolfe's second novel, *You Can't Go Home Again.* After Wolfe died, the townspeople relented, as they often do when a troublesome celebrity stops being troublesome and remains merely famous, and bought the house to turn into a memorial for him. It is now a North Carolina State Historic Site. Visiting the house, which has been kept the same as it was when the Wolfes lived in it and has descriptions from Wolfe's writing in appropriate places so you can compare the words with the reality, goes a long way toward explaining the often gloomy tone of his writing. Nominal admission fee. Open Monday through Saturday from 9:00 A.M. to 5:00 P.M. and Sunday from 1:00 to 5:00 P.M. Shorter hours and closed Mondays, November through March. Closed state holidays (704–253–8304).

Just about 10 miles outside Asheville, near Weaverville on Reems Creek Road off Highway 25 North, is another state historic site, the ◆ **Zebulon B. Vance Birthplace.** Vance was a Civil War officer, a U.S. senator, and governor of North Carolina. In fascinating contrast to the splendor of Biltmore Estate, this restored pioneer farmstead has only a five-room log house and some outbuildings. The log house was reconstructed around the original chimneys. The outbuildings, including loom house, spring house, toolshed, smokehouse, corncrib, and slave cabin, are furnished as they would have been between 1795 and 1840. Displays instruct you further in life of the times. Admission is free. Open April through October, Monday through Saturday from 9:00 A.M. to 5:00 P.M. and Sunday from 1:00 to 5:00 P.M. November through March, closed Mondays and open shorter hours other days (704-645-6706).

Asheville makes a good center from which to go in several different directions. Following the parkway takes you to **New River State Park.** A drive of about 20 miles down Interstate 26 takes you into the southern mountains, where Flat Rock, Hendersonville, and Saluda offer many rural pleasures and some interesting crafts and antiques shops. Driving northeast from Asheville along the Blue Ridge Parkway takes you higher into the mountains to Blowing Rock and environs. And a scenic ride east along Interstate 40 and Highway 226 to Polkville brings you back into the lower elevations of the Piedmont.

If you follow the parkway almost to the Virginia border, getting off to drive north on Highway 221, you come to the oldest river in North America and the second oldest (the Nile is older) in the world. It's the only major river in the country that runs south to north. Paradoxically called New River, it meanders peacefully through more than 100 miles of northwestern North Carolina. The name was the result of surveyors' surprise when they finally chanced upon the river they hadn't known about in this remote part of the state in 1749.

You enjoy good access to the river from New River State Park (919-982-2587), an area of breathtakingly lovely mountains, valleys, woods, and fields, 8 miles southeast of Jefferson off Highway 88 on State Road 1588. Compared to other state parks, New River shows up infrequently in travel books and articles, probably because it is in a remote part of the state and because the facilities are primitive. This is the river to find if you like placid canoeing rather than wild races through white water and want fishing spots not bothered by heavy powerboat traffic. There are canoe landings and campgrounds. The woods are great for hiking and are full of spots that cry out for a simple picnic.

Behind the peaceful scene lies the story of a dramatic struggle that isn't anywhere near being over. It started in the 1960s, when Appalachian Power Company planned to build a dam there, raising tremendous public objection. In protective response Congress designated the area a National Wild and Scenic River in 1976, effectively stopping the power company.

But little funding was ever forthcoming to actually buy and protect the land, and gradually a new force is changing the scene along the river: subdivision and development. New houses, roads, and lots are beginning to appear on what was farmland or woodland. There's even a golf course in the works. Although none of it is in the state park, of course, people who like their countryside bucolic and unspoiled are getting nervous, whereas those who value economic development for the area are digging in their heels and sending out the bulldozers.

Given the usual inclination of those who can afford to build in the prettiest places—high on mountain summits, on beaches and islands, and along rivers—it's hard to say what will happen along the New River in the coming decade. The good news is that the state park is, as locals like to call the river, "a national treasure" and should remain a special place to visit for a long time to come.

About thirty-five minutes north of Asheville, in Madison County, you find an interesting cluster of places near the **French Broad River.** This river is a step above the Nantahala River in difficulty for white-water rafting, but the water is warmer and far fewer users come into the area, so your experience is considerably more off-the-beaten-path than it is on the Nantahala. The greater part of Madison County is part of Pisgah National Forest, and the Appalachian Trail passes through the county, offering short segments of trail for day hikers. In the little town of **Hot Springs** you can soak in outdoor tubs along the banks of the river. Hot mineral water, flowing constantly from natural springs at a temperature of about 100 degrees, has often been considered therapeutic and is certainly relaxing, the more so if you indulge in a massage while you are there. Spa rates are figured by the hour and vary from $12 to $25, depending on the time of day. Massage rates are calculated by the half-hour and become proportionately slightly less expensive per half hour the longer the time you reserve. A thirty-minute massage is $25. For information about the hot springs and massages, phone (704)

622–7676. For information about white-water rafting tours, phone Carolina Wilderness (800–872–7437) in Hot Springs. For information about hiking, contact the Visitors Information Center at the Forest Supervisor's Office, P.O. Box 2750, Asheville 28802.

On the drive down Interstate 26, one of the most interesting stops is the ◆ **Carl Sandburg Home National Historic Site,** a 240-acre farm called Connemara, a bit south of Hendersonville in Flat Rock. Sandburg spent the last twenty-two years of his life here, mostly writing, while his wife and daughter managed the place as a goat farm. His collection of poems, *Honey and Salt,* was written here when he was eighty-five. The poems contrast with such earlier works as "Chicago," reflecting not only the work of an older man, but also of one living in different surroundings. For instance, in the poem "Cahokia," Sandburg writes about an Indian watching a butterfly rise from a cocoon, flowers sprouting in spring, and the sun moving. The Indian, Sandburg writes, doesn't worship the sun, but dances and sings to the "makers and movers of the sun." It takes on added significance when you know that Flat Rock was named for a large granite plateau that had once been a Cherokee sacred ground. Sandburg's life here was influenced not only by the early cycles of nature, but also by Cherokee Indian lore. Similarly, looking across the mountains, it's easy to understand how Sandburg might have arrived at his poem "Shadows Fall Blue on the Mountains."

When you visit Sandburg's study at Connemara, both the man and his poetry seem alive. The study is said to be exactly as he left it, with a shawl tossed over the back of his desk chair, a clunky manual typewriter standing on an upended crate, and stacks of paper and disorderly piles of books everywhere. A fascinating aspect of the entire home is the simplicity of its furnishings. To say the interior is plain puts it mildly. The furniture resembles what you find in a summer camp, functional but not decorative. Also fascinating is the fact that every room is crammed with books, all of which appear to have been well used. Similarly, the rooms where Helga kept records about breeding her goats are functional and were apparently furnished with no thought to decoration. What you find outside seems more carefully designed. You may also walk along trails on the grounds where you see the kinds of plants and wildlife from which Sandburg must have drawn many of his images. Nominal admission is charged. Open daily except Christmas from 9:00 A.M. to 5:30 P.M. Inquire about some special seasonal activities (704–693–4178).

Flat Rock has a wonderful place to enjoy a good dinner and spend the night. **Highland Lake Inn,** on Highland Lake Drive, is a complex with a lodge, cabins, and cottages scattered on a wooded property that also has a lake, an olympic-sized swimming pool, and 100 acres of walking trails. The Lindsey family dream was to create a self-sufficient compound, and although they haven't managed that entirely yet, they've come close. The restaurant serves vegetables and herbs organically grown on the property, bread baked from organic wheat stone-ground in the inn's kitchen, and eggs from free-range chickens. The food is simply wonderful. Offerings range from something as simple as a chicken pot pie with a puff pastry crust to some elaborate pasta and seafood dishes and lamb with lime sauce. Every bite you take bursts with flavor. If you are traveling with children, this is a place where you can take them to see how to take an egg out of a chicken nest, see vegetables growing in a garden, and watch a goat being milked. Phone (704) 693–6812 or (800) 762–1276.

From Flat Rock you can head over onto Highway 176, driving about 12 miles to **Saluda,** a little town of less than 1,000 people, with a notable concentration of antiques and artisans. Walking around in the little town itself, you find several shops selling local crafts and antiques and a general store run by a pair of women reminiscent of the sisters on *The Waltons* television show, except, of course, they aren't offering Mason jars full of the "recipe"—as far as anyone knows.

Saluda has two overnight possibilities, quite different from one another. At the top of a steep hill, overlooking Saluda's main street, Dottie Eargle's **Woods House** has six rooms, including one in a separate cottage. The place is furnished throughout with late Victorian and turn-of-the-century antiques, highlighted by an outstanding collection of old needlework displayed throughout the inn. Dorothy has run an antiques shop for many years, and she has the ability to put together a room as only those intimate with antiques and their earlier uses can. (She cooks breakfast in a real country kitchen that has a wood-burning stove.) The inn (704–749–9562) is open April through October. In the center of town, Dorothy has a real estate office, now grown to three rooms, entirely furnished with antique oak office furniture. If you admire those old, functional oak file cabinets, bookcases, and desks and chairs, it's worth a trip to Saluda just to see the office.

A few miles into the country, in a totally different mood, **The Orchard Inn** (800–581–3800) sits atop the Saluda rise on eighteen wooded acres at an elevation of 2,500 feet. Owned and operated by Veronica and Newell Doty, this place is filled with beautifully arranged antiques, art, and books, and, of course, has a spectacular view from every side. The inn has two excellent chefs. One does magical things with trout and beef, and so on, emphasizing flavor and presentation without relying on heavy, fatty sauces. The other makes breads and desserts that have guests raving. All this food is served on a glassed-in porch that overlooks the Warrior Mountain Range.

When you call these Saluda telephone numbers, be patient. Sometimes the little local phone company has problems; always through the ringing you hear burbles and rasps like something out of the days of hand-cranked phones, and you feel that a very young Aunt Bea should answer.

THE HIGH COUNTRY

The next drive you might make from Asheville continues north on the Blue Ridge Parkway to ◆**Mount Mitchell State Park,** elevation 6,684 feet, the highest point in the eastern United States. You'll leave the parkway at milepost 355.4 to take Highway 128 to the 1,500-acre wilderness park. It's a 5-mile drive to the peak, but it will feel a lot longer. The park has hiking trails, picnic areas, a visitors center with maps, camping areas, and a lookout tower from which you can see what must be the most stunning mountain views east of the Mississippi. There are also a restaurant and a refreshment stand. Be careful while you're here. Mount Mitchell is named for Dr. Elisha Mitchell, who fell off the summit and died. Your falling off too probably wouldn't lead to getting the mountain renamed in your honor. The park is closed in winter (704–675–4611).

The next step you might try along the parkway is at milepost 331, where Highway 226 and State Road 1100 take you to Emerald Village near Little Switzerland. At Emerald Village, established on the site of the Old McKinney and Bon Ami mines, you can visit the **North Carolina Mining Museum,** which displays the tools used at the height of gem mining in the area. Outdoor displays and a printed trail guide explain the entire mining process, and you have the opportunity to look for your own emeralds, rubies, aquamarines, and the like. More vigorous all-day tours through mines not previously open to the public, complete with hard hats, rock hammers, and a chuck-wagon lunch, are available at scheduled times. If your gem hunting doesn't go well, you can pick up something at the shop or have a rough gem cut, polished, and set into a piece of jewelry. Other attractions include a fluorescent mineral display, railroad items, and a craft shop. Open from 9:00 A.M. to 5:00 P.M., May 1 through October 31. Open an hour longer in the evening from Memorial Day to Labor Day (704–765–6463).

From here you could return to the parkway or go north on Highway 221 to get to ◆ **Linville Caverns** and Linville Falls, just beyond the caverns. If you're back on the parkway, exit at milepost 317.4 and turn left on Highway 221. Linville Caverns lie under Humpback Mountain and were believed to be have been forgotten by the white race until about 100 years ago, when fish that seemed to be swimming out of the mountains caught the attention of explorers. During the Civil War, deserters from troops on both sides hid in the caverns. Today the caverns are lit electrically, showing stalactites and stalagmites and trout that, having always swum in the dark, can't see. Guides lead the tours 2,000 feet underground, pointing out important features and answering questions. A modest admission fee is charged. Open June 1 through Labor Day from 9:00 A.M. to 6:00 P.M. Closed at 5:00 P.M. in April, May, September, and October and 4:30 P.M. in March and November. Open weekends only in December, January, and February; closed Thanksgiving and Christmas (704–756–4171).

Linville Falls comprises two waterfalls at Linville Gorge and a primeval canyon in the sizable wilderness area given to the Blue Ridge Parkway by John D. Rockefeller. The gorge is the deepest cut east of the Grand Canyon. There are hiking trails and picnic spots.

Still moving north along the parkway, you come to ◆ **Grandfather Mountain,** where, if you've got the nerve for it, you can walk across the **Mile-High Swinging Bridge,** a 218-foot suspension bridge between two peaks that sways in the wind. Should you quite sensibly prefer to put your feet on something more solid, Grandfather Mountain has lots of hiking trails. You'll need to pick up a moderately priced permit and a trail map at the entrance. This is the area where the **Scottish Highland Games,** open to the public, are held the second weekend in July every year. It is also a spot that attracts hang gliders. Open from 8:00 A.M. to dusk summers; closed at 4:30 P.M., sometimes earlier, in winter. Admission is $9.00 for adults, $5.00 for children aged four to twelve. Please phone (704) 733–4337 or (800) 468–7325.

A few minutes farther on Highway 221 brings you to the ◆**Blowing Rock,** a cliff 4,090 feet above sea level that overhangs Johns River Gorge, 3,000 feet below, at the town of Blowing Rock. Because of the way the gorge is shaped and overhung, air blows upward, making snow appear to fall upside down and throwing upward light objects tossed over the edge. According to the legend of Blowing Rock, a Cherokee brave leaped to his death here to keep his tribe from making him return to the plains, leaving his Chickasaw wife behind. She prayed to the Great Spirit until the sky turned red and the wind blew her brave back up onto the rock. A wind has blown up from the valley ever since. A moderate admission is charged. Open from April through Octo-

The Tweetsie Railroad

ber, 8:00 A.M. to 8:00 P.M., weather permitting; 9:00 A.M. to 5:00 P.M. the rest of the year (704–295–7111).

By the time you get to Blowing Rock, the children will probably have heard of ◆ **Tweetsie Railroad,** a family theme park that has been operating in North Carolina since 1956. It's touristy but kind of fun. Coal-fired steam engines pull the train of open cars through 3 miles of staged events: a train robbery, an Indian raid, and so on. Also, a chair lift carries you up to Mouse Mountain, where you can pan for gold and walk through the petting farm. Another section of the park duplicates a country fair of the early 1900s, right down to the cotton candy. Among other features are an ice cream parlor, a jail, and a firehouse. Moderately high admission is charged. Open daily from Memorial Day through October from 9:00 A.M. to 6:00 P.M., with shorter hours and some features closed weekdays after Labor Day. The days and hours of operation here can, as one employee put it, "change at any time," so do call ahead (704–264–9061 or 800–526–5740).

Blowing Rock has several places to spend the night, including the long-popular **Green Park Inn** (704–295–3141) and the newer **Meadowbrook Inn** (704–295–3141). Meadowbrook Inn has 46 rooms and serves continental breakfast, lunch, and dinner. You are also just 8 miles south of Boone, a commercial resort area where you'll find lots of motels, which, though out of spirit with the off-the-beaten-path traveler, are easy and comfortable when you're tired and just need to sleep. A more romantic place, **Gideon Ridge Inn** (704–295–3644), a small inn with eight guest rooms and a fireplace, is becoming known for its cozy rustic interior and good breakfasts.

When you have more energy, save it to drive on up into **Valle Crucis,** close to Boone but totally unlike it in nature. Although the little town sees hundreds and hundreds of visitors, it manages to continue operating and looking like a small town. Its history dates back to 1780, when Samuel Hix, the first known white settler in Valle Crucis, staked a claim to 1,000 acres. Later he traded the land for a gun, a dog, and a sheepskin. Eventually it became an Episcopal mission, named *Valle Crucis* because three creeks came together in the shape of a cross. Today the mission serves as a retreat for many church denominations.

People stop most often at the ◆ **Mast Store,** an authentic general store listed on the National Register of Historic Places, which still sells penny candy, seeds, leather boots, Woolrich sweaters, flannel shirts, long johns, and about everything else you can think of, mostly stacked, not too neatly, along wooden shelves. The store has begun sending out a mail-order catalog reminiscent of early L. L. Bean.

The ◆ **Mast Farm Inn,** not associated with the store, is just outside the village on State Road 1112 (704–963–5857). Francis and Sibyl Pressly cater to overnight guests and to folks who make reservations for dinner. Mast Farm is also on the National Register of Historic Places, as a restored, self-contained mountain homestead, comprising a spring house, icehouse, washhouse, barn, blacksmith shop, gazebo, and cabin, in addition to the inn. Sleeping here is quiet and comfortable. The antiques are sparingly arranged to avoid a sense of clutter. Eating here is an experience in socializing as well as in tasting. Before dinner, Francis learns a little something about each of the guests and, as he seats them at the long dining room tables, introduces everyone. People chat back and forth throughout the meal, passing platters and talking about their backgrounds and travels. The food goes way beyond standard southern cooking. Each dinner includes, along with the meat and vegetables, a meatless entree. When they serve a roasted pork loin, the meat is separated from the ribs for slicing, and the bones are passed separately for gnawing. Seasonal vegetables come from the farm gardens. Brown bagging is permitted in case you like beer or wine with a good meal.

THE FOOTHILLS

Instead of heading north from Asheville, you may choose to start east toward the foothills and the Piedmont. A drive of about 40 minutes on Highway 74, heading southeast from Asheville takes you to the little vacation community of ◆ **Lake Lure.** Everything centers on the 1,500-acre lake, which has 27 miles of shoreline. The area is surrounded by the Blue Ridge Mountains. It's in the heart of the thermal belt, where the climate is almost always a bit milder than the extremes of heat and cold in the rest of North Carolina. The temperate climate makes Lake Lure excellent for boating, fishing, hiking, and horseback riding year-round.

Sterling Stables (704–625–9009) at nearby Gerton offers rides that pass waterfalls and streams and a 25-mile view of Strawberry Gap. On weekends they also offer riding lessons and often have cookouts. The people here are known for their good humor and entertaining rides.

For hiking, you have your choice of hundreds of trails. Organized hikes leave from **Chimney Rock Park** (704–625–9611 or 800–277–9611), located on U.S. Highway 64/74 in Chimney Rock, a private park with hiking trails, easier paths, and even an elevator to the top. From the top you can look down and see Lake Lure and mountains in all directions. Hickory Nut Falls, one of the highest waterfalls in the East, is on the grounds. The park is open daily from 8:30 A.M. to 7:00 P.M. from mid-April through October and from 8:30 A.M. to 6:00 P.M., November to mid-April. In bad weather the park closes. Admission is $9.00 for adults, $4.50 for children aged six to fifteen. For simpler hiking you can ask almost any local person to recommend a favorite trail. These personal favorites are loosely kept secrets because no one wants them to become overrun with lookey-loos and littered with aluminum cans, but locals gladly share the information with anyone who cares enough to ask personally.

Bob's Marina, open every day of the week year-round, rents boats and tosses in information about the best fishing spots for free (704–625–4522).

For a more gossipy, less strenuous ride, 28-foot pontoon showboats leave every half-hour from the pier beside the beach in the center of town. The tour follows the shoreline and the guide shows you where *Dirty Dancing* and several other movies were filmed, talks about the history of the lake, and tells stories of some strange local lore (704–625–9323).

For total relaxation, in comfortable lodgings with good company and a spectacular view, try the ❖**Lodge on Lure Lake** (704–625–2789 or 800–733–2785), the only lodge directly on the lake. The massive stone fireplace and lakefront dining room and porch create a quintessential country inn atmosphere where rocking and reading seem like the most appropriate activities of the day. The lodge was originally built as a hideaway for the North Carolina Highway Patrol in the 1930s. Stories of the shenanigans of those years add to the fun of the place, as do Jack and Robin Stanier, the good-humored innkeepers. Robin's expansive breakfasts are good enough to have earned a place in several cookbooks and make you full enough to skip lunch.

For dinner, the **Point of View Restaurant** (704–625–4380)

takes its name from its location on a stony point overlooking the lake. It's less than half a mile from the lodge, so you can walk to it easily. In this rustic setting the service is casual and friendly. The menu includes mountain trout, a rack of lamb specialty, seafood, and Continental-style entrees. All spirits are served. The restaurant's hours vary and the place is popular, so it's a good idea to make a phone call before you go.

You're first attracted by the music coming through outside speakers. When you get inside, they'll play lots more music for you. You may hear the music from their independent record albums, *The Strayaway Child,* and *Heartdance.* The shop sells a highly personal selection of other tapes and albums, mainly hammered dulcimer music, piano music, and Celtic music. The shop is light and airy, with instruments on the walls, a fuel-efficient wood-burning stove, and a mountain rocker. You're invited to sit down and try any of the instruments or listen to the recorded music. If you're interested and ask, you can almost always manage to be shown through the workshop area and have the whole process explained to you. Open from 10:00 A.M. to 5:00 P.M. Monday through Saturday (704–669–7675).

Just a few miles from Lake Lure, at Bat Cave, **Hickory Nut Gap Inn** (704–625–9108) offers mountaintop lodging in an atmosphere that the proprietors, B. and E. Z., call "laid back." This inn, built in 1950 as a mountain retreat for a wealthy businessman, has four guest rooms and a suite, all with private baths. Each room is paneled with a different kind of wood: cherry, poplar, black walnut, red oak, white oak, and, in the closets, cedar. The great room has a cathedral ceiling and a stone fireplace. One of the guest rooms has a fireplace as well. The decor is a mix of Native American arts and crafts, foreign oddities, and such unlikely wall decorations as a handwoven dress that B. wore back in her hippie days. Breakfasts venture far beyond the standard egg dishes and often include specialties such as polenta and black beans, though B. will always provide more traditional fare if you want it. From here it's an easy drive up either Highway 74A or State Road 9 to Interstate 40 where you find **Black Mountain,** an interesting village that was once a Cherokee Indian center and now is a thriving community specializing in all kinds of top quality arts and crafts. The town has taken to calling itself "The front porch of Western North Carolina," a name that seems to suit the peaceful but interesting atmosphere of the community.

In May and October Black Mountain sponsors the Mountain Music Festival, during which musicians play the old mountain music on dulcimers, fiddles, bagpipes, and mandolins. In August the Sourwood Festival features more music and dancing and a large arts and crafts show. These events are fun; they're also well attended, so if you have any notion of being in Black Mountain when they occur you will need to arrange for lodging well ahead of time. **Black Mountain Inn** (704–669–6528) is a small place at 718 Old Highway 70 with six guest rooms. The building was once a studio and retreat where artists and writers such as Norman Rockwell and John Steinbeck spent time. The decor is casual country, the breakfasts are buffet-style, with home-baked breads and homemade granola. **Monte Vista Hotel** (704–669–2119), 308 West State Street, has both food and lodging in a cozy environment typified by antiques, a stone fireplace, and old-time southern cooking. The hotel has thirty-six guest rooms, with hardwood floors, antiques, and chintz. The dining room serves three meals a day, featuring everything from biscuits to southern fried chicken to ambrosia. Breakfast is served from 6:45 to 10:00 A.M., lunch 11:30 A.M. to 2:30 P.M., and dinner from 5:00 to 7:00 P.M.

Visiting the ◆**Song of the Wood,** at 203 West State Street, a workshop and salesroom devoted to dulcimers and unusual string instruments and their music, leaves you feeling exhilarated and refreshed. Jerry Read Smith makes hammered dulcimers and the even more unusual bowed psaltery, a small triangular instrument played with a violin-type bow, similar to a medieval bowed harp. JoAnn, Jerry's sister, manages the showroom. Everything about the shop is devoted to keeping the old music alive, producing fine-quality handmade instruments, and surrounding you with music.

As for shopping, the streets are lined with crafts shops, antiques shops and antiques malls, and a craft co-op. For instance, on Cherry Street, **The Seven Sisters Gallery and Shop** (704–669–5107), is notable for its fine selection of pottery, jewelry, fiber art, wood crafts, and glass art. This shop is open from 10:00 A.M. to 5:00 P.M. Monday through Saturday, 1:00 to 5:00 P.M. Sunday. On State Street, **The Phoenix** (704–669–4045) has a colorful assortment of blown glass, stained glass, fused glass, jewelry, and pottery. It is open Monday through Friday from 10:00 A.M. to 5:00 P.M., and Sunday from noon to 4:00 P.M. And on Sutton Avenue the **Old Depot** (704–669–6583), a nonprofit arts and crafts center of the Swannanoa Valley, is located in the old Southern Railway Depot. The building, constructed in 1893, was turned into a crafts center in 1976. Classes, demonstrations, and crafts sales are all held here. The center is not open in the winter and hours in spring, summer, and fall may vary, so call ahead.

Sometime during your visit to Black Mountain, stop at **Mountain Bar-B-Que Restaurant** (704–669–7078) for barbecue and iced tea or one of their other items. This is a simple little place, almost incongruous in its distinctiveness, surrounded by fast-food chain eateries. In this eatery, with its red-and-white checked tablecloths, where most of the customers seem to know each other, the people who work behind the counter are friendly, and the barbecue is really good. The restaurant is open from 11:00 A.M. to 9:00 P.M. Monday through Saturday and 11:00 A.M. to 4:00 P.M. Sunday. Closed Sundays in November.

Immediately after Black Mountain, you come to **Old Fort,** an area that was still considered Cherokee Indian land for some time after white pioneers began pushing in during the middle 1770s. At the beginning of the American Revolution, General Griffith Rutherford assembled 2,500 troops to attack the Cherokees, who seemed to be siding with the British. Afterward, the Indians conceded a huge portion of land, a pattern that was repeated often up to the time of the Trail of Tears in 1838. In subsequent years, the Western North Carolina Railroad became important here. The **Mountain Gateway Museum** tells the story, as do the Stepp and Morgan cabins that were moved here later. The site is a branch of the North Carolina Museum of History. It's not a big, splashy place and deserves your attention for that very reason. Admission is free. Open daily from 9:00 A.M. to 5:00 P.M. and Sunday from 2:00 to 5:00 P.M. (704–668–9259).

An outdoor treat in the same area is the **Catawba Falls Trail,** a special place that Eleanor Brawler wrote about for the *Charlotte Observer.* The main falls are the headwaters of the Catawba River. You'll find Catawba River Road at the Old Fort exit off Interstate 40. Follow the road through 3 miles of farmland, where you'll come to a small bridge and a private road at a tree farm. Cross the street to the right bank, walk past an old dam about a mile on, and when the path ends, cross the stream again, to the left bank. Here you should be able to hear the falls, and you'll come to a trail and then a clearing, where you'll find the waterfalls, falling from 220 feet above you. If you're hesitant about hiking into unfamiliar territory, ask in town for advice. Local people know the area.

Brawler suggests a second, shorter hike in the Falls Branch area, to see falls so little known they aren't even named. At Marion, go north from Interstate 40 on Highway 221/226, crossing the Catawba River and passing the River Breeze Restaurant. Drive 5½ miles after crossing the river. Turn left at the Woodlawn Motel and continue on 0.8 mile. The paved road ends. Bear left at the fork on a dirt road far enough to park. At the little bridge, you'll find a trail to the right that wanders through the rhododendrons beside a mountain stream. At the next fork, bear left again to see the falls. The area is also rich in wildflowers.

After these adventures, return to Interstate 40 and drive on to where Highway 226 intersects Interstate 40 at Glenwood. From here, you can enjoy a beautifully scenic drive to Polkville while you also enjoy a good brisk sit. This is one of the prettiest drives in the state.

From Polkville, you might want to take a quick drive north on Highway 10 into the little village of ◆ **Casar**—pronounced *KAYser,* population about 340. It's a place you'd never know about unless someone told you. Elizabeth Sturgeon, a woman well under fifty who was raised here, remembers every quaint detail. The people who founded the town meant to call it "Cae-sar," but somehow they got the spelling wrong, and it's been Casar ever since. Until recently, all the major roads were dirt; even today they are not all paved. When the roads came into the center of this little spot, a stop sign stood—most of the time. Every Saturday night one old gentleman who didn't navigate too well when he was in his cups (homemade 'shine—it was a dry area) ran into it and knocked it down. Every Monday morning, someone put it up again.

Even into our high-tech age, Casar has been a place where electricity, telephones, and indoor plumbing were frills, luxuries nobody wanted. Hamburgers and hot dogs were unknown. Today, Elizabeth estimates, 95 percent of the people have power and plumbing. You still could have trouble over the hamburgers and hot dogs with the older folks.

In the center of town you can see what used to be Tom Hoyle's grocery store, where he accepted eggs and chickens in payment for flour and other merchandise.

The school used to serve grades one through twelve and have a phenomenal basketball team. School started early in the season and closed for six weeks during cotton-picking time because all the children, generally ten to twelve to a family, were needed to work in the fields you see around the school. Elizabeth still has her cotton-picking sack. If you look behind the school, you can find the place on the bank where the kids ran down to the store to buy penny suckers with coconut in them.

Elizabeth doesn't live in Casar any more, but she goes back often and finds it only a little changed—more modern in its technology, but the same warm little place as far as its people go. Park your car and walk around awhile. Elizabeth says, "You might get looked at, but somebody will come to see if you need help."

Somehow, Art Linkletter found out about this area and started a golf resort called **Pine Mountain Lake** about 7 miles on toward Morgantown. Certainly you could get a hamburger in the restaurant there, but the resort hasn't tainted Casar one bit.

When you return to Polkville, pick up Highway 182 to Lincolnton and then Highway 150 on to Mooresville, a town of about 9,000 people, where you can find the necessities of traveling in a congenial environment. Shortly after you pass through Mooresville, still on Highway 150, you'll come to ◆**Carrigan Farms,** a place worth visiting any time of year. By the road in front of rows of greenhouses in a large shelter, you can buy asparagus and hanging baskets in April, strawberries in May and June, fresh vegetables all summer, cider and pumpkins in October, and poinsettias in November and December. Growing produce and plants, with twenty-five people employed, this farm is an effort of Doug and Susan Carrigan, his parents, and his grandparents. Yet this is more than a family farm; it's a farm involved in the community in ways that make you feel good, even though you live somewhere else. For instance, the walls are covered with letters and drawings from school kids who've visited the farm.

Dear Susan and Doug,

Susan, we liked the hayride.
We also liked the way the cow thought your finger was a bottle.
Doug, we liked the way you showed us the honey bees.
We had fun.

Love,
Matthew
Adam
Karen
Michael

Hang around to talk with the people, breathe the clear country air, and pick up whatever is in season. If you call ahead at the right time of year, you can probably even arrange a hayride (704–664–1450).

GENERAL INDEX

Entries for Inns, Bed and Breakfasts, and Potteries will appear in the special indexes beginning on page 130.

Inns and Bed and Breakfasts

Potteries